A Theological Understanding of Power for Poverty Alleviation in the Philippines

American Society of Missiology
Monograph Series

Chair of Series Editorial Committee, James R. Krabill

The ASM Monograph Series provides a forum for publishing quality dissertations and studies in the field of missiology. Collaborating with Pickwick Publications—a division of Wipf and Stock Publishers of Eugene, Oregon—the American Society of Missiology selects high quality dissertations and other monographic studies that offer research materials in mission studies for scholars, mission and church leaders, and the academic community at large. The ASM seeks scholarly work for publication in the series that throws light on issues confronting Christian world mission in its cultural, social, historical, biblical, and theological dimensions.

Missiology is an academic field that brings together scholars whose professional training ranges from doctoral-level preparation in areas such as Scripture, history and sociology of religions, anthropology, theology, international relations, interreligious interchange, mission history, inculturation, and church law. The American Society of Missiology, which sponsors this series, is an ecumenical body drawing members from Independent and Ecumenical Protestant, Catholic, Orthodox, and other traditions. Members of the ASM are united by their commitment to reflect on and do scholarly work relating to both mission history and the present-day mission of the church. The ASM Monograph Series aims to publish works of exceptional merit on specialized topics, with particular attention given to work by younger scholars, the dissemination and publication of which is difficult under the economic pressures of standard publishing models.

Persons seeking information about the ASM or the guidelines for having their dissertations considered for publication in the ASM Monograph Series should consult the Society's website—www.asmweb.org.

Members of the ASM Monograph Committee who approved this book are:

William P. Gregory, Associate Professor of Religious Studies, Clarke University

Susan L. Maros, Affiliate Assistant Professor of Christian Leadership, Fuller Theological Seminary

RECENTLY PUBLISHED IN THE ASM MONOGRAPH SERIES

Sue Whittaker, *Music and Liturgy, Identity and Formation: A Study of Inculturation in Turkey*

William A. Coppedge, *African Literacies and Western Oralities?: Communication Complexities, the Orality Movement, and the Materialities of Christianity in Uganda*

A Theological Understanding of Power for Poverty Alleviation in the Philippines

With Special Reference to US-Based Filipino Protestants in Texas

Yohan Hong

FOREWORD BY
Gregg A. Okesson

American Society of Missiology Scholarly Monograph Series 57

☞PICKWICK *Publications* · Eugene, Oregon

A THEOLOGICAL UNDERSTANDING OF POWER FOR POVERTY ALLEVIA-
TION IN THE PHILIPPINES
With Special Reference to US-Based Filipino Protestants in Texas

American Society of Missiology Scholarly Monograph Series 57

Pickwick Publications
An Imprint of Wipf and Stock Publishers
199 W. 8th Ave., Suite 3
Eugene, OR 97401

www.wipfandstock.com

PAPERBACK ISBN: 978-1-6667-0679-6
HARDCOVER ISBN: 978-1-6667-0680-2
EBOOK ISBN: 978-1-6667-0681-9

Cataloguing-in-Publication data:

Names: Hong, Yohan, author. | Okesson, Gregg A., foreword.

Title: A theological understanding of power for poverty alleviation in the Philippines : with special reference to US-based Filipino protestants in Texas / by Yohan
Hong ; foreword by Gregg A. Okesson.

Description: Eugene, OR: Pickwick Publications, 2022 | American Society of
Missiology Scholarly Monograph Series 57 | Includes bibliographical references
and index.

Identifiers: ISBN 978-1-6667-0679-6 (paperback) | ISBN 978-1-6667-0680-2 (hard-
cover) | ISBN 978-1-6667-0681-9 (ebook)

Subjects: LCSH: Poverty—Philippines—Prevention. | Missions—Philippines. |
Religion and sociology. | Immigrants—Texas.

Classification: BV3380 H66 2022 (print) | BV3380 (ebook)

02/22/22

I dedicate this book to those who have
taught me the true meaning of power.

To my parents, the late Rev. Sabon Hong, and Deokja Han:
Thank you for your unconditional love, prayers, and support.

To my lovely daughter, Esther:
You are God's most wondrous treasure in my life.
You'll never know how much I love you.

To my eternal friend and loving wife, Jenny:
You have patiently stood by my side with endless prayers,
timeless encouragement, and sacrificial support.
Your life and ministry showcase how to use
the divine power of love.

Contents

Acknowledgments

MOST OF ALL, I give all my thanks, honors, and glories to God who is the ultimate source of power and has empowered me to participate in His redeeming work for the transformation of this broken world through this study.

I would like to thank many people, to whom this book is indebted. First and foremost, I owe a great debt of gratitude to Dr. Gregg Okesson who has been incredibly gracious and encouraging to me, inspired me with sage guidance, and showcased the divine use of power.

I further thank two Filipino American Protestant Churches and their pastors in Texas, especially all the individual participants in my interviews, who graciously welcomed me into their churches and homes, taking the time out of their busy schedules to sit with me, share their life stories with me, and endured my questions. Their passion, desire, and commitment to transform their homeland the Philippines just fascinated me. Without their supports, this book would ultimately not have been possible.

I am also deeply indebted to the North Alabama Annual Conference of the United Methodist Church, including Bishop Dr. Debra Wallace-Padgett, Rev. Dale Cohen, Rev. Kelly Clem, Rev. Sheri Ferguson, Terry McElheny, J.D., Rev. Stephen Fincher, and Rev. Joseph Riddle. Without their prayers, loving care, and timely support, I could not have completed this academic journey.

Moreover, my special thanks go to everyday people in Bulacan and Davao of the Philippines, who gave me inspiration, insight, and motivation through their candid sharing of life stories. Their despair, struggle, tear, laughter, hope, love, and faith are the very rich foundation of this book.

I trust and pray that God will use this book to raise up people who are willing to be the hands and feet of Jesus to bring about the transformation of the broken world. "Father, Your Kingdom come, Your will be done on earth, as it is in heaven." Amen.

Foreword

MIGRATION IS DRAMATICALLY RESHAPING our world. Movement of people is not a new phenomenon in human history. However, the sheer size, scope, and speed of migration we are experiencing today confronts us with new dynamic realities. As people move, they negotiate their new context through a complex dance of adaptation, revision, and translation. Scholars attempt to understand these dynamics by speaking of first generation, 1.5, second, and third generation immigrants; as well as analyzing the relationships they maintain with their home context through transnationalism. These are complex dynamics and don't come pre-packaged to us in a one-size-fits-all typology. Thus, in order to study migration, we need sensitive yet critical ethnographic research into specific diaspora populations. That is what we enjoy in this book.

Yohan Hong boldly enters into these dynamics. He takes the reader on a fascinating journey into the different ways US-based Filipino immigrants negotiate power dynamics in holistic mission. It is a beautifully written narrative that foregrounds and honors the voices of the immigrants themselves in the process of understanding mission in the diaspora. The book is descriptive before it is prescriptive. Much of the beauty we are currently enjoying in World Christianity is taking place precisely through such movement. This book narrates that story.

Hong was a missionary in the Philippines. He carries those missionary sensitivities into his research taking place amongst US-based Filipinos. The book wades thickly into power dynamics, trying to understand how these immigrants interpret and negotiate power in the US. While

Hong is sensitive to avoid interpreting everything as power; he takes power dynamics seriously and convincingly demonstrates that we cannot understand diaspora agency without looking at how they interpret power. The study focuses upon two aspects of power: structural and mythic. He explains how these two aspects should not be interpreted as distinct from each other, but his study demonstrates how Filipino diasporas move fluidly between the two in a holistic sense.

While this book provides high caliber sociological insights, Hong is at his best when integrating sociology with theology. He shows us that the US-based Filipinos move between the two, and thus we cannot appreciate their agency without likewise entering into the spirited dance that combine their social and religious worlds.

I warmly recommend this book.

Gregg A. Okesson, PhD

1

Introduction and Research Methodology

IN 2006, I WALKED down a street in Manila, the Philippines' capital. One girl holding a baby with sad eyes approached me and said, "Give me one dollar." It did not take long for me to notice that there were plenty of boys and girls begging on the street. Anthony, a second grader in an elementary school in Bulacan, asked me on the street to buy a bundle of *sampaguita*, the national flower. Daisy, a student of Bulacan State University, had only one meal a day due to lack of money. In Cainta Rizal, a number of people die of dengue fever every year because they do not have money to buy medicine, not enough money even for one pill. While serving as a missionary in the Philippines from 2006 to 2010, I continuously wondered, "Why is there such a huge gap between the poor and the rich?" To my eyes, the reality of everyday people with a low socio-political-economic status was so devastating. The poor seemed incredibly poor and powerless while the rich seemed extremely wealthy, privileged, and powerful. Statistics also verify the devastating reality of the Philippines: 41.5 percent of the national population survive with less than $2 a day as of 2009 and the highest 20 percent of the total population dominate almost the half (49.7 percent) of the entire income in the Philippines as of 2012.[1] Almost half of the total population in the Philippines survive on less than two dollars a day. I sensed that something had been going wrong in the system of politics, economics, and even the mentality of people. In Bulacan, a suburb of Manila (capital), I had a chance to talk with a tricycle[2] driver about his son staying

1. World Bank, "Income Share Held by Highest 20%."
2. Motorized tricycles, or simply tricycles are an indigenous form of the auto rickshaw

with him during the day, asking "why didn't you send your son to a school today?" He answered me, "I don't allow him to go to school." I asked him back, "For his better future, your son needs to study." He stared at me for a while and then started to say something surprising: "I know his destiny. He will be a tricycle driver just like me." It seemed that poverty is a choice of individuals.[3] Beth, an English teacher in Makati, shared with me her bitterness toward the Philippines, saying "our young college graduates are being sold to foreign call centers at a price of $200 a month." Beth resented the disastrous reality of the Philippines where the government cannot guarantee employment for young people to work and dream of their better future in their home country. She blamed this situation on the government and corrupt political leaders, pointing out this issue as a structural problem, rather than an individual's choice. Thus, understanding poverty seemed to be a never-ending task; poverty continues to defy simplistic descriptions, definitions, and easy solutions.

One prevailing sense regarding poverty that I received as an outsider in the Philippines was that "everyday people"[4] with a lower socio-economic-political status communicated some expression of powerlessness. I encountered many of them saying that they feel powerless, blaming the elite and the government for poverty and inequality, and consequently perpetuating their image of powerlessness. I also heard people saying "*Bahala na*," which generally means "what will be will be" or "I don't care," in a way that seems to hint at fatalistic feelings of hopelessness, when they are confronted with challenging situations.

Through these expressions of powerlessness, I found out that poverty is not just a matter of individuals' lack of material resources; poverty also has social and cultural dimensions. Poverty needs to be understood in the concept of power because everyday people communicate a sense of powerlessness within their day-to-day relationships. Moreover, every relationship

---

and are a common means of public transportation in the Philippines. These public utility vehicles either ply a set route or are for-hire, like taxis.

3. In the Philippines, it is said that tricycle drivers generally earn at least PHP 300 per day, which is equivalent to $5.72 as of 2018. This profession cannot provide enough money for everyday people to survive or support their family. The reason I asked him about educating his son was because in the context of the Philippines, education plays a significant role as the number one factor toward promoting people's status in society and helping them get out of poverty.

4. I use the term "everyday people," instead of the poor, in order to avoid pejoratively labeling the poor. Refer to my definition of poverty in the section Power and Poverty in chapter 2.

is a power relationship whereby power is perceived, negotiated, and exercised by everyday people. Within these power relationships, everyday people experience deprivation, powerlessness, physical isolation, economic poverty, and all other characteristics of poverty. In effect, people are poor and powerless because "there are large-scale practices and a whole system of social roles, often firmly approved by the members of society generally, that cause or perpetuate injustice and misery."[5] The way we understand the nature and causes of poverty tends to determine how development responds to poverty. In this sense, how to perceive, understand, negotiate, and exercise power in everyday life is a crucial key to approach the issue of poverty, and even alleviate it.

Considering various causes of powerlessness, I questioned how the Protestant Church in the Philippines should view its role in transforming the lives of those experiencing powerlessness.[6] The Philippine Statistics Authority reported in October 2015 that 80.58 percent of the total Filipino population are Roman Catholic, 10.8 percent are Protestant and 5.57 percent are Islamic.[7] In the context of the Philippines, compared to the Catholic Church, the Protestant Church tends to be considered a minority. According to Philippine Council of Evangelical Churches (PCEC), despite the unprecedented growth in number of Filipino Evangelical churches for the last 30 years (from 4,900 in 1975 up to 77,000 as of 2011), they seem limited in engaging social issues like the oppressive power structure, corruption, and injustice. It proved true that the Philippines had been perceived to be the most corrupt in the Asia-Pacific Region.[8] Dr. Cesar Vicente P. Punzalan, Deputy National Director of PCEC, stated:

> We do not fully understand nor attempted to recognize and deal with structural evil: the lack of national righteousness, the lack of social peace, the lack of public justice, and the lack of economic sufficiency as the whole body of Christ . . . . 86% of our churches do not have enough resources, organizational sustainability, or community impact; 13% are healthy having the capacity to engage

---

5. Wolterstorff, *Until Justice and Peace Embrace*, 24.

6. In this study, I do not distinguish between the two different terms of "the Protestant Church" and "the Evangelical Church." Rather, I will intentionally use the Protestant Church to indicate both forms of Christianity. Therefore, if I refer to the Protestant Church, this term is used to contrast with the Catholic Church.

7. "Philippines in Figures: 2014, National Statistics Office."

8. Davao City Ministerial Fellowship on June 13, 2011.

in impact-driven ministry; 1% have more capacity for impact to transform the nation and engage in international missions.[9]

Overall, this analysis represents that Evangelical churches have little or no influence as salt and light in society. In fact, the churches are called to transform lives in the Philippines, but many of them have been the objects that need to be transformed. In the words of Walter Brueggemann, these churches appear to be assaulted and co-opted by "the consciousness and perception of the dominant culture" around them,[10] which robs them of "the courage or power to think an alternative thought."[11]

Furthermore, I recognized the necessity of understanding power theologically especially in the context of the Philippines. The spiritual dimension of power should be developed to explain why social systems become oppressive, exploitative, and self-serving even though good people try to make social institutions do what they are supposed to do. The Philippines is known as one of the most religious ones and the third largest Catholic country in the world. Many everyday Filipinos I met were able to interpret and articulate their situations theologically by using sacred words such as "If God willing," "God will take care of us," or "This is my destiny from God." I also found out that religious leaders and the Church (mainly Catholic Church), along with political leaders, tend to be regarded as one of the powerful groups with some negative connotations. Some people even depicted religious leaders as gluttonous, greedy, and privileged ones. Moreover, as religion in the Philippines has roots in colonial history arising out of the colonization by Spain (Catholicism) and the United States (Protestantism), it needs to be more deeply investigated through the history of the Philippines.

STATEMENT OF THE PROBLEM

My hypothesis is that everyday people in the Philippines communicate a sense of powerlessness. Filipino Protestant Churches should be able to provide a consciousness and perception alternative to the sense of powerlessness and function as an alternative community that brings about transformation. To achieve this goal, I suggest that Filipino Protestant churches, while continuing to empower themselves and find their own

9. Davao City Ministerial Fellowship on June 13, 2011.
10. Brueggemann, *Prophetic Imagination*, 3.
11. Brueggemann, *Prophetic Imagination*, 39.

assets and resources in the Philippines, need to cooperate with US-based Protestant Filipinos who were born and lived in the Philippines, and then migrated to the United States because they know the reality of the Philippines objectively, criticize the dominant consciousness and perception on power in the Philippines, and energize them by some alternative perspectives and tangible supports. For this reason, this study sought to figure out how US-based Protestant Filipinos could be agents of transformation in the Philippines. Furthermore, the missional agency of US-based Protestant Filipinos has been seldom investigated in the academia of Diaspora Missiology, especially regarding how they perceive power structures and a sense of powerlessness in the Philippines, how they exercise power in their everyday life, and how they can contribute to the transformation of the Philippines in tangible ways.

RESEARCH QUESTIONS

This study sought to answer the following research questions:

Research Question 1

How do US-based Filipino Protestants in Texas perceive, and understand power structures in the Philippines? What do they think gives power?

Research Question 2

What Filipino cultural values or worldviews do US-based Filipino Protestants in Texas view as causing and perpetuating a sense of powerlessness in the Philippines?

Research Question 3

How do US-based Filipino Protestants in Texas perceive, negotiate, and exercise power? How do they respond to their missional calling to transform the lives in the Philippines?

Research Question 4

What theological meanings do US-based Filipino Protestants in Texas give to power?

DELIMITATIONS

First, this study limits the scope of poverty to a sense of powerlessness in the perspectives of development studies. In development studies, scholars and practitioners have defined poverty in many different ways such as poverty as deficit, poverty as entanglement (Robert Chambers), poverty as lack of access to social power (John Friedmann), poverty as diminished personal and relational well-being (Isaac Prilleltensky), poverty as disempowering system (Jayakumar Christian), and poverty as a lack of freedom to grow (Ravi Jayakaran).[12] The major focus of this study in understanding poverty is on a sense of powerlessness of everyday people in the Philippines.

Second, this study seeks a holistic understanding of power as a means of transformational development in order to overcome a sense of power-lessness of everyday people in the Philippines. There are several different understandings of the causes of poverty: physical, social, mental, and spiritual. In traditional development studies, the spiritual area of poverty has been neglected. The nature of poverty, however, is fundamentally relational, and the cause of poverty is fundamentally spiritual. For enhancing a holistic understanding of poverty, this study explores structural evil and social imaginary that cause and perpetuate a sense of powerlessness. For transforming the sense of powerlessness of everyday people, a theology of power is presented in as a reference to the redeemed power.

Third, the research objects in this study are confined solely to US-based Filipino Protestants; neither Filipino Protestants in the Philippines nor Filipino Catholics in the United States are included. This study aims to examine and discover the missional agency of Filipino American Protestants for the transformation of the Philippines. In this process, the perspectives of Filipino American Protestants on power structures and social imaginary in the Philippines were explored. The group included those who were born, raised and educated in the Philippines, immigrated to the United States, and had lived in the States for more than five years. This number is not an absolute criterion, but a potentially good duration for the immigrants to be aware of socio-political-economic structures of the United States and be able to compare the differences and similarities of socio-political-economic power structures between the Philippines and the USA.

Fourth, the participants in the ethnographic research should be fluent in speaking both English and Tagalog. This bilingual capability is the major

12. Myers, *Walking with the Poor*, x.

condition for the cultural brokers and cultural changers in two different cultures (see the case of the *ladinos* discussed in the later chapters).

Fifth, research focused on two different Filipino American Protestant Churches in Texas, the United States: one in Dallas area and the other in Houston. These churches were randomly selected for this research and the names cannot be mentioned to keep confidentiality of the data collected. They belong to different denominations, have different leadership styles in terms of governing system, and have different characteristics of Filipino communities. These differences with many other similarities made the research more reliable and complementary. Moreover, Texas has been one of the most preferable destinations for Filipinos to immigrate.[13]

DEFINITION OF KEY TERMS

Filipino American Immigrants

Since this study seeks to empower Filipino American Protestants to be agents for the transformation of the Philippines, I needed to know first how they came to the United States and who they are. The history of Filipino immigration to the United States has five different phases: during the Spanish rule, during American colonization, Post-Independence, Post-Immigration and Nationality Act of 1965,[14] and 2001 to the Present. The colonial experience of the Philippines with the United States had a profound impact on Philippine migration. The first significant migration of Filipinos to the States began from the second phase, that is, during American colonization. In this phase, the first Filipino immigrants were *Pensionados*,[15] the children of rich influential Filipinos, sent to study and work for the U.S. Armed Forces during World War I and II, and *Manongs* and *Sakadas*,[16] Filipino contract laborers who worked as farmers in the sugar plantations of Hawaii,

---

13. Cherry, *Faith, Family, and Filipino American Community Life.*

14. Remigio, "Demographic Survey of the Filipino Diaspora," 27–29.

15. According to Merriam-Webster Dictionary, a *Pensionado* is "a Philippine student whose expenses are paid by the government while he or she studies aboard." Merriam-Webster, "Pensionado."

16. A *manong* is a Filipino term reserved usually for a person older than you (e.g. your older brother, your grandfather, your older cousin, etc). *Manongs* refer to laborers who migrated to the United States to work in plantations in the 1930s; *Sakadas* means lower-paid workers recruited out of the area. In Hawaii, the word is synonymous with these pioneers who came to seek their fate for a better life for themselves and their families.

Washington and California, and as canners in Alaska.[17] This pattern of Filipino immigration to the States continued until the third phase of Post-Independence from 1946 to 1965. The fourth phase commenced when the 1965 Immigration Act was passed, which officially committed the United States to accepting immigrants of all nationalities on a roughly equal basis. This increased Filipino immigration to the United States. Thereafter, the profile of Filipino immigrants to the States began to tremendously change with the influx of Filipino immigrant professionals such as nurses, medical doctors, medical technologists, and teachers. As of 2016, according to the Migration Policy Institute (MPI), Filipino immigrants in the States (1,942,000) rank fourth in number, surpassed by Mexico (11,575,000), India (2,435,000), and China (2,130,000).[18] What does this statistic imply? Why do Filipinos leave the Philippines and then move to the United States? What is their missional calling to transform their homeland Philippines and how have they responded to this calling? Chapter 5 answers these questions in light of Diaspora Missiology and Missional Agency.

Everyday People

I use the term *everyday people*, instead of "the poor," in order to avoid pejoratively labeling the poor. In addition, defining the poor is a very complicated and multifaceted issue. For this reason, when I use the term everyday people, I point to the ordinary people, generally speaking, who comprise the basic sectors such as the farmers, workers, urban poor dwellers, students and professionals, having a lower socio-political-economic status than those who are known as the powerful and the rich. In the context of the Philippines, as figured out in chapter 3, it is obvious who the powerful and the rich are, that is, the ruling elite class that originated from landowners throughout the colonial period[19] and constituted a national oligarchy during the late 1980s.[20] Therefore, the term *everyday people* does not open up doors to the idea that even rich people are everyday people in some aspects of their lives. Rather, I would use the term everyday people in this study as the abbreviation of "everyday people with a lower socio-political-economic status."

---

17. Clement, *Running Head,* 20–22.

18. Migration Policy Institute (MPI).

19. Clarke and Sison, "Voices from the Top of the Pile," 219.

20. Anderson, "Cacique Democracy in the Philippines," 3–31.

Powerlessness

In this study, I argue that everyday people communicate a sense of power-lessness. What does powerlessness mean? I define powerlessness as lack of ability, influence, or authority to control crucial aspects of their lives. If so, what does power mean? I simply define power as the capability to get things done regardless of exterior resistance or restriction (For the further under-standing of power, see the section of power theories in chapter 2). What does, then, powerlessness look like? David Stravers, a former missionary to the Philippines, encapsulates the worldviews of the poor in the Philippines into three factors: the sense of powerlessness, the commitment to the status quo, and the perception that outside forces will always be in control.[21] They are interrelated with one another and concurrently represent the charac-teristics of powerlessness altogether. For example, if times are really bad, a poor Filipino in Murica[22] may tell that his or her life is "*pigado gid*," that is, "so full of troubles that there is nothing one can do to escape them."[23] Therefore, one can only say "*amo ina sa amon kabuhi*," that is, "the way it is and there is nothing we can do about it."[24] In Negros Island, people are "pressured to not seek to change the status quo by acquiring too much good or by transgressing the boundaries of his or her assigned status."[25] If one person receives too much relief from outside, other members of the community may "become hostile against him or her through gossip and ostracism."[26] Thus, in this context, someone's acquiring wealth means de-priving someone else. Since the issue of powerlessness is multi-faceted in its definition, cause, and solution, this study chose to focus on two major causes for powerlessness: structural evil and social imaginary.

Structural Evil

In this study, I define structural evil as the asymmetric structure of socio-political-economic systems that cause and perpetuate powerlessness. Given the context of the Philippines, structural evil is represented by oppressive

---

21. Stravers, "Poverty, Conversion," 335.

22. Murcia, officially the Municipality of Murcia, is a municipality in the province of Negros Occidental, Philippines. See the official site of Negros Occidental Government.

23. Stravers, "Poverty, Conversion," 336.

24. Stravers, "Poverty, Conversion," 336.

25. Stravers, "Poverty, Conversion," 336.

26. Stravers, "Poverty, Conversion," 336.

and corruptive political power structures (the patrimonial oligarchy, patron-client relations, elitism, and a cacique democracy), and exploitative economic power structures (booty capitalism and neo-patrimonialism). Chapter 3 discusses structural evil in greater detail.

Social Imaginary

Charles Taylor defines social imaginary as "the ways people imagine their social existence, how they fit together with others, how things go on between them and their fellows, the expectations that are normally met, and the deeper normative notions and images that underlie these expectations."[27] In social imaginaries, people perceive a common understanding, conduct common practices, and discern a sense of legitimacy. I argue that the powerlessness of everyday people in the Philippines has become "a sense of the normal expectations" and "the kind of common understanding" that enable them "to make up their social life."[28] This hints that the sense of powerlessness functions at the mythic level as some kind of social imaginary. Chapter 4 explores two different Filipino cultural values (*Bahala na* and *Utang na loob*) as social imaginaries that cause and perpetuate a sense of powerlessness.

Colonialism

A sense of powerlessness in the Philippines cannot be understood without the concept of colonialism. The term colonialism refers to "a scenario in which a state or group has power over another territory and its people."[29] Simply put, colonialism means "the policy and practice of a power in extending control over weaker peoples or areas."[30] Michael Rynkiewich explains, "The modern era of colonialism has involved the expansion of Europe and Japan through trade (state or private corporations), military conquest, forced eviction, resettlement, cultural imperialism, and economic exploitation of local populations, lands, and resources."[31] The practice of colonialism typically encompasses "the development of political policies used to dominate or control a subjugated people and geographic

---

27. Taylor, *Modern Social Imaginaries*, 23.

28. Taylor, *Secular Age*, 172.

29. Mercadal, *Salem Press Encyclopedia*, 2.

30. Dictionary.com, "Colonialism."

31. Rynkiewich, *Soul, Self, and Society*, 184.

area, the occupation of the territory with settlers, and the economic exploitation of the territory."[32]

The Philippines was colonized by Spain (1521–1898) and the United States (1898–1946). Colonialism in the Philippines immensely affected Filipinos' lives, cultures, worldviews, politics, economics, and religion. In the case of religion, Christian missions by Catholic missionaries during Spanish colonization and Protestant missionaries during American rule carried out their mission works under the influence of colonial power. For this reason, religious leaders, especially Catholic leaders, throughout Filipino history tend to be labeled as a privileged powerful elite group. Contemporary socio-political forms like clientelism, oligarchy, and elitism in the Philippines are originally attributed to colonialism. Especially, the land-based economic system throughout colonization ushered the appearance of "neo-patrimonialism" in the Philippines in the early 21st century. Moreover, the economic expansion of the United States to the Philippines resulted in re-colonialization of the Philippines economically and culturally. Preference for American cultural and material products, such as music, films, clothes, and food, gradually replaced the preference for local products. The American educational system and the use of English as the major language played a significant role in the continuing process of re-colonization.

Transformation

In this study, I use the term transformation to indicate one of the ultimate conditions by which everyday people overcome powerlessness. Simply put, whereas I define poverty as powerlessness, development is defined as empowerment. In addition, I suggest that empowerment of everyday people is possible through transformation. Vinay Samuel states, "Transformation is to enable God's vision of society to be actualized in all relationships, social, economic and spiritual, so that God's will may be reflected in human society and his love be experienced by all communities, especially the poor."[33] Samuel clarifies the concept of transformation further: "Mission is individuals coming to Christ, challenging corrupt and sinful systems, structures and cultures and enabling individuals and communities to experience God's transforming power."[34] Transformation is here located by identifying Christian action against sin and God's power as a transforming power.

32. Mercadal, *Salem Press Encyclopedia*, 2.

33. Samuel and Sugden, *Mission as Transformation*, 227.

34. Samuel, "Mission as Transformation," 243.

The Protestant Church

The Protestant Church traditionally represents one of the three great divisions of Christianity: the other two are the Roman Catholic Church and the Eastern Orthodox Church. Historically, Protestantism began during the Renaissance as a protest against the Roman Catholic Church. In the Protestant Church, its major distinctive divisions are the Mainline Church, the Evangelical church, and the Pentecostals. In this study, however, I do not distinguish between these different terms. Rather, given that the Roman Catholic Church dominates the religious context of the Philippines, I will intentionally use the Protestant Church to indicate these three different forms of Christianity, which do not fall into the category of the Catholic Church. In other words, the word the Protestant Church will be used to contrast with Catholic Church.

RESEARCH METHODOLOGY

In order to explore the answers to the research questions, I used an integrative literature and ethnographic interview methodology. My literature research prepared the theoretical foundations on the major themes of this study, and then I engaged in the conversation between the literature and the data collected from my ethnographic interviews, in such integrative ways to analyze, test, and evaluate.

Ethnographic Interview

My ethnographic subjects were Filipino American Protestants in Texas because this study sought to empower them to be agents of transformation in the Philippines. I used ethnography as the primary means of collecting data in the churches. Julian Murchison describes ethnography as follows:

> Ethnography is a research strategy that allows researchers to explore and examine the cultures and societies that are a fundamental part of the human experience. Unlike many other scientific strategies, the ethnographer as researcher is not typically a detached or uninvolved observer. The ethnographer collects data and gains insights through firsthand involvement with research subjects or informants. With few exceptions, the ethnographer conducts research by interacting with other human beings that are part of the

study; this interaction takes many forms, from conversations and interviews to shared ritual and emotional experiences.[35]

To conduct ethnographic research, ethnographers can and do employ a number of different methods and techniques such as participant-observation, interviews, focus group, and maps and charts.[36] At the stage of designing my ethnographic research, I planned interviews and focus group as the major methods. However, considering the sensitivity of my research topic, and some Filipino cultural values such as *hiya* or shame, I realized in my first focus group that it was not appropriate for me to collect personal information, experience, and story about powerlessness in the setting of a group discussion. Hence, for this study, I mainly chose to employ individual interviews as the major key method. This was the only thing that necessitated me to make a change. Murchison states, "Interviews and conversations are almost certainly a key component of a research design for historical recollections or personal perspectives."[37] In other words, I collected data and gained insights about a sense of powerlessness of everyday people in the Philippines, through firsthand interviews and interactions with Filipino American Protestants who were born and raised in the Philippines and then immigrated to the United States.

Generally speaking, there are two types of interview: the formal and the informal.[38] For the informal interview, I attended a church retreat in order to build relationships with my informants, and also had meals with some key informants to help talk about their own stories in more flexible and comfortable settings. It was easy for me to start a conversation with my informants because Filipinos are well known as people who are hospitable, friendly, outgoing, and easy to befriend. I was confident that face-to-face personal interviews and conversations were the most effective way for me to collect data. Such methods operated well within Filipino contexts due to their strong "smooth interpersonal relations" (SIR). The formal interview may be either structured or unstructured. The structured interview "makes use of a prepared interview schedule, a series of questions to which the researcher requires specific answers."[39] In an unstructured interview, it is

---

35. Murchison, *Ethnography Essentials*, 4.
36. Murchison, *Ethnography Essentials*, 40.
37. Murchison, *Ethnography Essentials*, 40.
38. Crane and Angrosino, *Field Projects*, 57.
39. Crane and Angrosino, *Field Projects*, 59.

usually best to "begin with the broadest, most open-ended questions, then fill in with specifics as one's own knowledge of the topic grows."[40]

For conducting my ethnographic interviews, 31 participants were chosen out of two different Filipino American Churches in Texas (16 participants in Dallas, and 15 in Houston) with consideration given to gender and age. It is necessary to collect diverse voices regarding the research topics. By gender, 16 women and 15 men participated in this research. By age, they consisted of 1 person in the 30s, 10 in the 40s, 12 in the 50s, 6 in the 60s, and 2 in the 70s. Most of my respondents were older because the majority of them had come to the United States during the earlier time of the fourth phase (from 1965 to 2000s) of Filipino immigration to the States. See chapter 5 for further information about this.

Considering the seriousness of the topic, I began most interviews with informal questions in casual conversation about their life story and immigration history, such as "How long have you stayed in the United States?" and "Why did you choose Texas as your destination?" Then, I slowly moved into combined unstructured and structured interviews with three main questions in addition to four or five sub-questions for clarifying and specifying their answers. Most of the questions make up a series of open-ended questions related to power: "What is the first impression when you hear the word power?" "What gives power to people?" "Who has power in your church?"

One of the primary goals of ethnography is "to access insiders' perspectives."[41] In other words, it is to see and understand the research topic through the eyes of the people being studied. In conversation and interviews, I was able to gain explicit knowledge, obtain detailed explanations and rationales as well as background information, and then ask for clarification or follow up on things observed or explained previously.[42] In this sense, "interviews were not just one-way interrogations, but interactions and conversations" which I was part of.[43] Furthermore, interviews were not only collecting the details of data, but also the process of testing the accuracy of details from multiple sources such as observations, and reading materials (books and articles). All formal interviews were recorded and later

40. Crane and Angrosino, *Field Projects*, 58.

41. Murchison, *Ethnography Essentials*, 44.

42. Murchison, *Ethnography Essentials*, 44.

43. Blommaert and Jie, *Ethnographic Fieldwork*, 43.

transcribed in full detail. At the same time, I took cursory notes on paper that would later be transcribed and highlighted in greater detail.

ANALYTICAL FRAMEWORK

Once the data and insights from the interviews were collected, I analyzed them through four steps of Critical Contextualization: Phenomenological Analysis, Ontological Reflection, Critical Evaluation, and Missional Transformation.[44] For exploring and analyzing the data collected from the ethnographic research, I used power theories for ontological reflection, a theology of power for critical evaluation, and diaspora missiology for missional transformation (see Table 1 and Figure 1).

The first step is to phenomenologically study power structures in the Philippines, and power perceptions (power and powerlessness) of Filipinos, through ethnographic interviews with Filipino American Protestants. In this process, I began by learning to see the world as the people I served do. It was important for me to reserve judgment until I was able to "fully study and understand the categories, assumptions, beliefs, worldviews, and logics the people used, and then understand how these shaped the way they think."[45]

Table 1. Four Steps of Analytical Framework

<Step 1> Phenomenological Analysis	<Step 2> Ontological Reflection	<Step 3> Critical Evaluation	<Step 4> Missional Transformation
Through ethnographic interviews	Through Power Theories	In the light of a Theology of Power	In the perspectives of Diaspora Missiology

The second step is to ontologically reflect on the collected data from ethnographic research, by exploring, projecting, and analyzing them through power theories like power-over, power-to, power-with, and power-within (see the section of Literature Review below). In this process, the "objective reality" of powerlessness was tested. Chapter 3 and chapter 4 have an

---

44. Hiebert et al., *Understanding Folk Religion*, 22.
45. Hiebert et al., *Understanding Folk Religion*, 22.

extensive description on how the objective reality of powerlessness in the Philippines is reflected by the power theories.

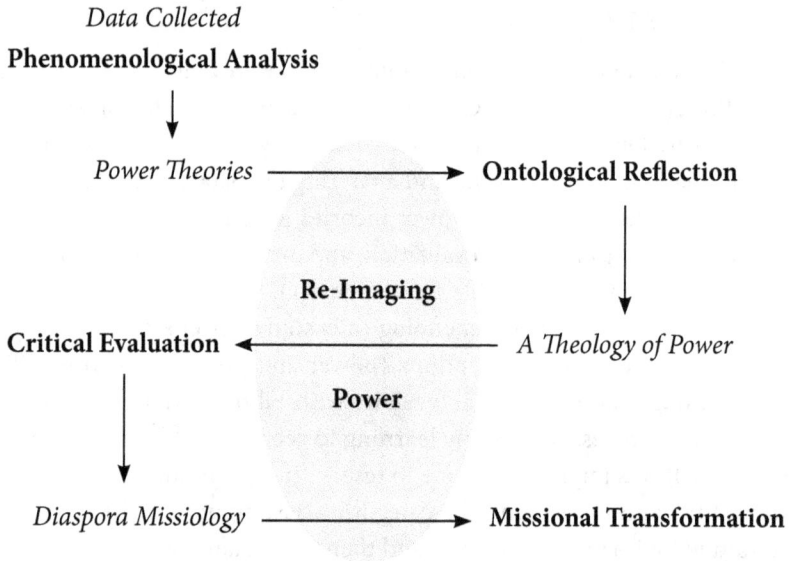

Data Collected

Phenomenological Analysis

↓

Power Theories ⟶ **Ontological Reflection**

↓

Re-Imaging

Critical Evaluation ⟵ *A Theology of Power*

↓

Power

Diaspora Missiology ⟶ **Missional Transformation**

Figure 1. Four Steps of Analytical Framework

The third step is to critically evaluate the collected data in the light of a theology of power (see Literature Review in chapter 2). This process is very significant in a way to figure out the alternative models that are biblically based and theologically sound. In the endings of chapter 6, I conclude by offering a critical evaluation on two major causes of powerlessness, in light of a theology of power.

The fourth step is to bring about missional transformation. Through the lens of Agency Theory and Diaspora Missiology, this study explored the potential models of "mission through" and "mission by/beyond" Filipino American Protestants for the transformation of the Philippines. Diaspora Missiology shed light on the missional agency of Filipino American Protestants.

THEORETICAL FRAMEWORK

Transformational Development

The term transformational development reflects my ultimate goal for this study. According to Bryant L. Myers, transformational development seeks "positive change in the whole of human life materially, socially, psychologically and spiritually."[46] Therefore, in transformational development, we need to explore not only the external causes that interplay "between the physical and social causes of poverty," but also "the largely internal contribution to poverty resulting from mental and spiritual causes."[47] This understanding helped the entire frame of this study: chapter 3 discusses the external causes of powerlessness and chapter 4 explores the internal contributors to powerlessness. Chapter 3 reveals and tackles socio-political-economic-religious structures which cause and perpetuate a sense of powerlessness, and therefore, need to be transformed. Moreover, chapter 4 challenges Filipino socio-cultural-psychological practices which also cause and perpetuate a sense of powerlessness. Furthermore, chapter 5 deals with this issue of powerlessness in a spiritual point of view, that is, Diaspora Missiology and Missional Agency, and then showcases how everyday people can transform these structural evils and fatalistic cultural practices not only by their faith and spiritual power but also by their organizational networks. This spiritual perspective is also supported by a theology of power (described in chapter 2), and some theological understandings of power by different scholars, like Robert Linthicum and Walter Wink (refer to chapter 2). In this regard, transformational development as a theoretical framework underlies this entire chapter of the study.

In the adjective transformational, we are reminded, "True human development involves making choices, setting aside that which is not for life in us and in our community, while actively seeking and supporting all that is for life."[48] Thus, transformation implies "changing our choices."[49] I believe that the word *choice* includes an implicit meaning of how to use power or agency. For this reason, the transformation of a sense of powerlessness starts from recognizing the different choices in wielding power, and discerning which choice empowers or disempowers everyday people.

---

46. Myers, *Walking with the Poor*, 3–4.

47. Myers, *Walking with the Poor*, 15.

48. Myers, *Walking with the Poor*, 15.

49. Myers, *Walking with the Poor*, 15.

For this purpose, this study offers some extensive descriptions about what kinds of power are in play (refer to power theories in chapter 2), how the fallen powers can be named and made visible (see chapter 3 and 4), and then ultimately the ways through which power should be transformed (chapter 3, 4, and 5).

Myers asserts, "The goals of transformation are to recover our true identity as human beings created in the image of God and to discover our true vocation as productive stewards, faithfully caring for the world and all the people in it."[50] Based on this point of view, I set up the goals of this study: to help everyday people in the Philippines discover true power in their identity as children of God and recover their true vocation as faithful and productive agents for transforming a sense of powerlessness. To achieve these goals, this study refers to the voices, perceptions, stories, and insights of US-based Filipino Protestants, by which this study seeks some positive changes in the whole of everyday people materially, socially, psychologically, and spiritually.

In the process of change, the critical question is, "Who will save us?" I would find the answer to this question in transformational development: "Transformational development journey belongs to God and to those who are on it, not to experts, donor agencies, or development facilitators. Whatever our framework or our methods, we must be willing to set them aside and let the poor discover their own way, just as we have done."[51] For this reason, this study sought to find a group of people who believe the transformative power of God and are willing to be the agents for transformation. In this study, Filipino American Protestants were presented as the transforming agents. Some people might conjecture that such a group could be found anywhere, even in the Philippines, who would fit this description. As chapter 5 describes, however, we cannot imagine the transformation of the Philippines without thinking of the existence of Filipino diasporas in the USA if we consider their continuous socio-political-economic impacts on the Philippines. Moreover, this study seeks to shine light upon the missional agency of Filipino American Protestants, which has been neglected in the academia of Diaspora Missiology.

The process of change should affirm the joint roles of God and human beings, God and the Church. Hence, in what follows, public theology will

---

50. Myers, *Walking with the Poor*, 3–4.

51. Myers, *Walking with the Poor*, 16.

be presented as one of the foundational theories for emphasizing the role of the church for the common good in everyday life.

Public Theology

For bringing about the transformation of powerlessness, the Filipino Protestant Church needs a better theology to balance public and individual interests, spiritual and physical realms of the Gospel. Based upon my experiences and observations as a missionary in the Philippines and also the words of the director of the Philippine Council of Evangelical Churches (PCEC) described earlier in this chapter, there has been a dichotomy in the church's understanding of the physical and spiritual realms. As a result, while people believe that "God's redemptive work takes place only in the spiritual realm," the socio-political-economic structures seem to be left to the devil.[52] In this regard, the term Public Theology has seemed an odd concept.

However, if the church is able to actively engage in public issues, it impacts how people perceive and deal with questions of public issues. The church's participation in the discourse on public issues can be "nurtured by theological thinking and academic discipline, but also by concrete experiences of political and ethical dilemmas."[53] Public Theology gives a plausible answer to this dilemma. Heinrich Bedford-Strohm asserts that the task of public theology is "to give orientation to the public in questions of ethical significance, and by addressing such questions of public interest it adds the flesh to the secular constitutional bones of a pluralistic society."[54]

In the context of the Philippines, I argue that the Protestant Church needs to be able to "bring the Christian faith into their political activism and moral reasoning in the name of a healthy democracy, and into their economic justice for the common good."[55] In this way, Public Theology can offer a theological framework of meaning and values that connect people in a society. Miroslav Volf maintains that Christian faith is "a prophetic faith that seeks to mend the world" and can bring into debate "a vision of human flourishing and the common good."[56] Thus, the Christian faith should

---

52. Myers, *Walking with the Poor*, 7.
53. Bedford-Strohm, "Tilling and Caring," 230.
54. Bedford-Strohm, "Tilling and Caring," 230.
55. Bedford-Strohm, "Tilling and Caring," 230.
56. Volf, *Public Faith*, xv.

be active in all spheres of life: "politics, economics, social relations, cultural values, art, communication, and entertainment and more."[57]

If Christian leaders or the Church are not able to voice out a prophetic faith in public spheres, "politicians are increasingly charged with the task of providing the bearings for a society's moral compass."[58] This fact verifies the need for the Filipino Protestant Church to be "the public church" that provides meaning, value for the common good to Filipino society where corruption of political leaders is rampant, where economics and the political process are dominated by the elite oligarchy, and where everyday people feel powerless. In other words, Filipino churches have not been able to function very well as society's moral compass. In this regard, the Church has to be "bilingual" in such a way that it is not only rooted in the specifics of Christian tradition but also seeks to "translate that into more publicly accessible language."[59] I believe this bilingual capability of the church is implicit throughout this study in dealing with the topics of powerlessness caused and perpetuated by structural evil (chapter 3) and cultural practices embedded in social imaginaries (chapter 4). In this regard, this study intends to be the bridge between the church and the world, human beings and God.

Public Theology grants legitimacy to why the Filipino Protestant Church in the Philippines and the U.S. should be able to put into practice a prophetic voice that would transform the asymmetric power of socio-political-economic structures in the Philippines. For this purpose, the Filipino Protestant Church in the Philippines should be the alternative community of love to the oppressive and exploitative structure of power represented by the elite oligarchy and the patron-client system that demarcate between public and individual interests. Public Theology will be one of the crucial tools to make the theology of the Church more appropriate to transform power in the world. I believe that transformed individuals can transform other individuals or the community, and then the transformed community can impact and initiate the transformation of the larger communities or social structures. Thus, this study places an emphasis on both individuals and communities as transforming agents. In this point of view, Public Theology has common ground with the Agency Theory presented in chapter 5. In Agency Theory, this study points out three different agencies

57. Volf, *Public Faith*, xv.
58. Graham, "Window on the Soul," 145.
59. Graham, "Window on the Soul," 145.

of Filipino American Protestants: individual agency, proxy agency, and collective agency. In the concept of collective agency, not only Filipino Protestants in the Philippines but also those in the USA are granted legitimacy as the part of the Church to exercise collective agency by engaging their Christian faith in public issues and striving to bring about the transformation of both socio-political-economic-religious structures and also cultural-psychological dimensions. In this regard, Public Theology along with Transformational Development as Theoretical Framework underlies this entire chapter of the study.

SIGNIFICANCE OF THE STUDY

To transform the Philippines, the system in the Philippines should be changed. We usually use the word *system* to "describe the political, economic, and value-creating functions of society."[60] If so, what do we mean by system exactly? Robert C. Linthicum gives an insightful definition of the word *system*: "A system is an organized body of people gathered together around three components: values that are held in common, structures that institutionalized those values, and individuals who manage and operate those institutions. Linthicum maintains, "All three components must exist for a system to be a system."[61] According to this definition, we recognize that a significant systemic change can occur only when individuals, structures, and values change. Therefore, we cannot imagine systemic change without transforming people. In the same manner, we cannot expect the transformation of people without transforming the articulated values of people. Likewise, we cannot also imagine transforming the values of people without systemic change because systems arise not just from what is seen, but what is unseen. Although these components are closely interconnected to one another, I realize that the role of human agents occupies center stage in this definition because a system ultimately designates an organized body of people. Therefore, our mission as Christians is to bring individuals to Christ, and concurrently to challenge corrupt and sinful systems, structures, and cultures so that individuals and communities will experience God's transforming power.

Therefore, one remaining question is, "Who can be the agents for that systemic change in the Philippines?" Based upon all the concerns and intentions described above, who can be the agents for the transformation of

60. Linthicum, *Transforming Power,* 24.
61. Linthicum, *Transforming Power,* 24.

the Philippines? Interestingly, I found a hint from the concept of the *ladinos* in the history of the Philippines. In this study, I argue that Filipino American Protestants are one of the contemporary forms of the *ladinos* who were cultural brokers, had been promoted to the upper-middle class during the colonization of Spain and the United States, and then consequently brought about some plausible structural changes in the Philippine society. I will make this stand out more in chapters 3 and 5.

CONCLUSION

This chapter laid the theoretical framework for showing the significance and direction of this study by dealing with my personal background, problem statement, research questions, and research methodology (data collection and data analysis). Moreover, the definitions of key thematic issues central to this study were introduced, such as everyday people, power/powerlessness, structural evil, social imaginary, transformation, colonialism, and the Protestant Church. This chapter sketched two major factors causing and perpetuating a sense of powerlessness in the context of the Philippines: structural evil and social imaginary. For Theoretical Framework, Transformational Development and Public Theology are presented and interwoven with other theories and contents of other chapters and provide the theoretical foundation which underlies the directions and goals of this study. In addition, this chapter highlighted the uniqueness of this study; a sense of powerlessness is investigated from the perspectives of Filipino American immigrants who were chosen as the informants for my ethnographic interviews.

In the following chapter, I review literature referred to for this study, theme by theme like power theories, power and poverty, powerlessness of Filipinos in the Philippines, Filipino immigrants to the USA and powerlessness, and A Theology of Power.

2

Major Themes of Discourse on Power

IN THE PREVIOUS CHAPTER, I introduced a sense of powerlessness as the key thematic issue. This chapter initially explores some scholarly writings central to this study, such as power theories, and the interconnectedness between power and poverty both in general and in the Philippines. These themes are highly convoluted matters, not easily comprehended or defined with clear boundaries. Nevertheless, they will be reviewed to a degree to provide some theoretical foundations for investigating and analyzing data collected from the research as described in the Analytical Framework of the previous chapter. The second half of this chapter focuses on a theology of power as the suggestive conclusion on which the concept of power (and powerlessness) is theologically examined and evaluated. This chapter gives rationale to my integrative methodology in dialogue between sociological and theological understanding of power.

POWER THEORIES

Power theories are the foundational tools in this study for interpreting, discerning, and analyzing the power structures in the Philippines and the power dynamics and power perceptions of everyday people, for the purpose of seeking the alternative models of power that are culturally appropriate, biblically based, and theologically sound. Gregg Okesson highlights, "especially in relation to sacralizing and/or secularizing currents at play with contemporary societies" like Filipino society, "it is important to look at power theologically and sociologically.[1] Andrew Walls also points out this aspect: "when theological studies cut themselves off from other branches of learning, they lost opportunities to renew their own streams with fresh, clear water."[2]

For this study, I basically adopt two general sociological understandings of power, that is, power-over and power-to, from *Comprehending Power in Christian Social Ethics* authored by Christine Firer Hinze who is a Christian ethicist. In addition to this, I will also introduce four types of power from Duncan Green in *From Poverty to Power*: power-over, power-to, power-with, and power-within. Green is the Head of Research at Oxfam in Great Britain, and prior to this position, worked as a senior policy advisor at the Department for International Development. While Hinze's categorization of power-over and power-to is a classical foundation of modern social theory in understanding power, Green's types of power offer more detailed categories of power including power-within and power-with, reflecting more contemporary and updated trend of power relations among the poor and rich countries in our globalized world. Finally, Robert Linthicum's types of power are also presented, with a particular emphasis on relational power (power-with). Since Linthicum has rebuilt poor urban communities through his church ministries, community organizations, and World Vision International,[3] his approach to power is ultimately more theological and biblical than that of Hinze and Green. The use of sociologists, a development specialist and a theologian in dialogue with the power types gives the rationale to my integrative methodology in this study. Linthicum's types of power offer a glimpse of how a theological understanding of power looks like, which is contrasted with a sociological typology of power other theorists hold. Green's four types of power are more of an integrative methodology that covers other theorists' types of power.

Power-over and Power-to by Christine F. Hinze

Hinze distinguishes the concept of power in two categories: power as "subordination" (power-over) and power as "effective capacity" (power-to).[4] According to Hinze, whereas the power-over model emphasizes "power's

1. Okesson, *Re-Imaging Modernity*, xv.

2. Walls, "Globalization," 78.

3. World Vision International is a Christian humanitarian aid, development, and advocacy organization.

4. Hinze, *Comprehending Power*, 5.

capacity to act *against* or *in spite of* others" (Max Weber and Karl Marx), the power-to model focuses on "power's efficacy as emerging *with* or *because of* others" (Michel Foucault, Hannah Arendt, Anthony Giddens).[5] In what follows, I will specify these two different understandings of power and interact with them.

SUBORDINATION (POWER-OVER)

First, power can be described as subordination (power-over). Power-over is hierarchical, structured, coercive, asymmetrical and dominating. This idea of power is at the heart of Max Weber and Karl Marx.

Max Weber. Max Weber was a German sociologist and political economist famous for his thesis of *The Protestant Ethic and the Spirit of Capitalism*, and for his ideas on bureaucracy. In general, Weber had a great reputation through critical confrontation with Karl Marx and Friedrich Nietzsche who were the international giants of 19th-century European thought.[6] In this regard it is interesting to compare Marx's perception of power with Weber's.

Weber had two definitions of power: *Macht* and *Herrschaft*. *Macht* is power as "probability that one actor in a social relation will be in a position to carry out his own will despite resistance, regardless of the basis on which this probability rests."[7] *Herrschaft* is power as "the probability that a command with a given specific content will be obeyed by a given group of persons."[8] In his definition of power, Weber presupposes that the use of legitimate force is inevitable and inescapable in human society in order to combat "the threats to individual freedom posed by modern bureaucratic power-over."[9] According to Wolfgang Mommsen, Weber's theory of power "is derived from the assumption that there is a fundamental dichotomy between qualified, i.e. charismatic leadership on the one hand, and the unreflected, submissive obedience of the governed on the other."[10] For this, there should be a premise to use: "the power of command does not exist unless the authority which is claimed by someone is

---

5. Hinze, *Comprehending Power*, 5.
6. Encyclopedia Britannica, "Max Weber."
7. Weber, *Economy and Society*, 53.
8. Weber, *Economy and Society*, 53.
9. Hinze, *Comprehending Power*, 26.
10. Mommsen, *Age of Bureaucracy*, 19.

actually heeded to a socially relevant degree."[11] Thus, Weber advocates for the use of charismatic domination of power for protecting individuals' freedom. In sum, Weber's understanding of power is basically "hierarchical, bureaucratic, and legal or rational domination."[12]

Weber's understanding of power also reflects an asymmetrical distribution of agency between commanders and followers.[13] Anthony Giddens makes the point: "Weber associated 'meaning' with *legitimacy.* Consequently, his account of bureaucracy is very much written 'from the top'; the ideal type of bureaucratic organization is heavily weighted toward how the 'legitimate order of a rational-legal form' is sustained."[14] Although Weber focuses on the legitimacy of power-over for protecting individuals' freedom and creativity, as empirically and historically known, many political leaders justify their use of *Herrschaft* with great visions for human flourishing, but end up with tyranny. We also have experienced many religious leaders who exercise *Herrschaft* using consecrated words for achieving personal benefits, which entails psychic or monetary coercion.

In this regard, in order to bring about and enhance the freedom of individuals, Weber's view should be complemented by a stress on power-to, identifying the values of freedom and creativity in effective collaborative efforts among the ordinary people. In the context of the Philippines, Filipinos learned the necessity that *Herrschaft* should be held in check by power-to, through their experience with the dictatorship of President Ferdinand Marcos under martial law from 1972 until 1981 and the People Power Revolution of 1986 against the regime's violence and alleged electoral fraud. However, one thing to keep in mind is that Weber is not making a normative claim about power. That is, Weber is not saying this is how power should be wielded. Rather, he is observing and theorizing about how power is wielded in these different kinds of social systems, whether it is appropriate or not.

Karl Marx. Karl Marx was a German revolutionary political sociologist and economist working during the 19th century. Marx with Friedrich Engels

---

11. Weber, *Economy and Society,* 2:948.
12. Hinze, *Comprehending Power,* 58.
13. Giddens, *Profiles and Critiques,* 205.
14. Giddens, *Profiles and Critiques,* 205.

published *The Communist Manifesto* in 1848, and *Das Kapital,* which later formed the basis of Marxism.[15]

Although the characteristics and consequences of modern industrial capitalism are the major motivation for both Marx's work and Weber's, Marx, unlike Weber, views the material (economic) sphere as the foundation that determines power dynamics in a society. For Marx, human societies develop through class struggle between the capitalist ruling class (the bourgeoisie) that "control the means of production" and the powerless working classes (the proletariat) that "enable these means by selling their labor power in re-turn for wages."[16] In this regard, Marx's description of socio-political power is "interest-oriented, structurist and asymmetrical."[17]

The notions of "alienation" and "ideology" are two crucial features of Marx's interpretation of the structures and power-over in capitalist po-litical economics.[18] Marx states, "The overturning and confounding of all human and natural qualities, the fraternization of impossibility–the *divine* power of money–lies in its *character* as men's estranged, alienating, and self-disposing *species*-nature. Money is the alienated *ability of mankind.*"[19] For Marx, in bourgeois capitalist society, money is the essential symbol of the degradation of humanity, thereby reducing human values to units of exchange. Marx's theory centers on "the alienation of persons from their products, their environment, and each other – in short, from their power of action and interaction – within class society."[20] In the view of Marxism, the state (bureaucracy) is always repressive and negative because it is a tool of the oppressor class. Marx's vision of the future communistic society is implied by a judgment that "dominative power-over is something destined to fall away and be replaced by a power of the people (power-to)."[21]

However, the only way for achieving this vision is through revolution by violence. This point of view gives justification to a *coup d'etat.* Moreover, Marx's class analysis falls into reductionism in a way to limit the causes of oppression mainly to an economic factor, neglecting other factors of so-cial problems such as sexual, racial, ethnic, and religious oppressions in

15. Encyclopedia Britannica, "Karl Marx."

16. Marx, and Engels, *Communist Manifesto,* 1–22.

17. Hinze, *Comprehending Power,* 39.

18. Marx, "Economic and Philosophical," 66–125.

19. Marx, "Economic and Philosophical," 104.

20. Hinze, *Comprehending Power,* 57.

21. Hinze, *Comprehending Power,* 43.

the glocal settings. In the case of Filipino Americans, even though they are away from the oppressive economic structure in the Philippines, they might feel powerlessness owing to multi-dimensional factors like racism, assimilation problems, identity crisis, familial-cultural conflicts, and inferiority resulting from a colonial mentality.

In sum, whereas Marx highlights "ideology, alienation, and the economic and class contradictions," Weber centers on "types of domination, legitimation, and the role of leadership in political power."[22] Regardless of whether or not people agree with the power theories of Weber and Marx, many people interpret the world through these lenses. Above all, the asymmetric structure of power under oppressive politics and exploitative economics in the Philippines can be understood by the concept of power-over. On top of that, I presume that power-over is not just a structural matter between the powerful and the powerless, but also an inter-personal issue among the relationships of everyday people in everyday life.

Effective Capacity (Power-to)

Power can also be defined as "effective capacity" (power-to), which means "primarily people's ability to effect their ends."[23] Power-to is "collaborative and non-hierarchical," which has "a countervailing stress on power as transformative capacity, rather than as super-ordination" (power-over).[24] According to Hinze, this analysis of power highlights "collaborative and mutually beneficial potentials of power that exclusively power-over treatments tend to overlook."[25] This idea is at the heart of Michel Foucault, Hannah Arendt, and Anthony Giddens.

Michel Foucault. Michel Foucault was a French philosopher, historian, social theorist, and "one of the most influential and controversial scholars of the post-World War II period."[26] Foucault's theories center on the relationship between power and knowledge, and how this relationship functions as social power in societal institutions. Foucault's analysis of power can be summed up by this sentence: "Power is everywhere; not because it embraces

---

22. Hinze, *Comprehending Power*, 61.

23. Hinze, *Comprehending Power*, 5.

24. Hinze, *Comprehending Power*, 107.

25. Hinze, *Comprehending Power*, 107.

26. Encyclopedia Britannica, "Michel Foucault."

everything, but because it comes from everywhere."[27] In Foucault's political thought, power is "a ubiquitous interaction called multitudinous relations of force by which the actions of people are produced, affected, and governed by other people."[28] Therefore, for Foucault, "power is a quality of collective interactions, not a possession of one or some."[29] For Foucault, society is a dynamic realm of power-over and power-to:

> If power were never anything but repressive . . . do you really think one would be brought to obey it? What makes power hold good, what makes it accepted, is simply that it doesn't only weigh on us as a force that says no, but that it traverses and produces things, it induces pleasure, forms knowledge, and produces discourse. It needs to be considered as a productive network which runs through the whole social body, much more than as a negative instance whose function is repression.[30]

Thus, Foucault recognizes that power is more of effective capacity, not simply a restrictive and constraining reality. Anthony Giddens also recognizes the significance of Foucault's position in this regard: "power, says Foucault, is not inherently repressive . . . Power has its hold because it does not simply act like an oppressive weight, a burden to be resisted. Power is actually the means whereby all things happen, the production of things, of knowledge and forms of discourse, and pleasure."[31]

Based upon his understanding of power as ubiquitous relations of force, Foucault perceives that "knowledge and power are integrated with one another"[32] and their interplay is not centralized or controlled, but is spontaneously spread in and through all the interactions of social relations.[33] Hence, Foucault states, "it is not possible for power to be exercised without knowledge; it is impossible for knowledge not to engender power."[34] For Foucault, thus, knowledge and discourses are all products and expressions of power relations.

27. Foucault, *History of Sexuality,* 1:94.

28. Hinze, *Comprehending Power,* 113.

29. Hinze, *Comprehending Power,* 111.

30. Foucault, *Power/Knowledge,* 119.

31. Giddens, *Profiles and Critiques,* 210.

32. Foucault, *Power/Knowledge,* 52.

33. Foucault, *Power/Knowledge,* 51–52.

34. Foucault, *Power/Knowledge,* 52.

Power for Poverty Alleviation in the Philippines

In this sense, perceiving specific networks of domination, Foucault presents one way of opposing oppressive disciplinary power-over, that is, "to release the oppositional power of discourses and knowledge that the ruling forces have submerged."[35] Foucault calls this "the insurrection of subjugated knowledges."[36] In the words of Kathy Ferguson, for Foucault, "opposition voices are a vehicle for bringing power to light as well as for altering that power."[37]

In the fallen world, human beings have been captured by the narratives that seem natural for the powerful to dominate and exploit the powerless. However, I believe that Foucault's understanding of power gives a rationale for Christians to convey the countervailing discourse, so as to alter the dominating story of power-over. Given that the socio-political-economic structures of power in the Philippines are oppressive and exploitative, Foucault's theory can be one of the ways to necessitate the need of the Word of God like a theology of power and the significant role of the church for transforming the world.

Hannah Arendt. Hannah Arendt was "a German-born American political scientist and philosopher known for her critical writing on Jewish affairs and her study of totalitarianism."[38] Arendt locates the source of power in "humans' capacity to act," since action always involves interaction that generates power structures that consist of a web of relationships.[39] For Arendt, it is speech and action that distinguish and constitute full human-ity: "A life without speech and without action . . . is literally dead to the world; it has ceased to be a human life because it is no longer lived among men."[40] Moreover, speech and action depend upon the plurality of human beings. In Arendt's estimation, plurality has a twofold character, that is, equality and distinction:

> If men were not equal, they could neither understand each other and those who came before them nor plan for the future and fore-see the needs of those who will come after them. If men were not distinct, each human being distinguished from any other who is,

35. Hinze, *Comprehending Power*, 123.
36. Foucault, *Power/Knowledge*, 81.
37. Ferguson, *Feminist Case*, 155.
38. Encyclopedia Britannica, "Hannah Arendt."
39. Arendt, *Human Condition*, 238.
40. Arendt, *Human Condition*, 176.

was, or will ever be, they would need neither speech nor action to make themselves understood.[41]

In the views of Arendt, only humans are capable of actually acting and speaking for themselves. In this sense, power is unleashed "when people act and speak in concert."[42] Thus, Arendt understands power as "a capability springing from and fostering communal connection."[43]

By insisting that power exists only in relations, Foucault is in agreement with Arendt. But Arendt rejects Foucault's further claim that power always directs and subjugates the actions of others. For Arendt, "authority, government, and their instruments are legitimate to the extent that they serve and protect public space and foster political action and power-to."[44] In Arendt's eyes, there is a good in human structures in a way that "public power can protect people" only because "it creates and maintains connections with them."[45] Moreover, while Weber and Marx focus on power as rule or superordination, Arendt locates power in the capacity of humans to speak and act together for mutually agreed upon purposes. Therefore, for Arendt, power is "never something possessed, but is only present in the process of political action"[46]: "Power corresponds to the human ability not just to act but to act in concert. Power is never the property of an individual; it belongs to a group and remains in existence only so long as the group keeps together."[47] Therefore, when someone is in power, this means that a certain group of people empowers this person to speak and act in their name.

Weber identifies effective social power with some form of hierarchy, or power-over. Michel Foucault's theory depicts power-over "not only as constitutive of social relations, but also as the source of power-to."[48] Here is the outstanding difference of Hannah Arendt from other theorists. Arendt argues, "power-to is constitutive of political life, and the necessary condition for all communal action, including coercive rule."[49] Arendt's focus is on how government can genuinely serve and foster power-to. In Arendt's

41. Arendt, *Human Condition*, 175–76.
42. Hinze, *Comprehending Power*, 139.
43. Hinze, *Comprehending Power*, 146.
44. Hinze, *Comprehending Power*, 142.
45. Hinze, *Comprehending Power*, 147.
46. Hinze, *Comprehending Power*, 132.
47. Arendt, "On Violence," 143.
48. Hinze, *Comprehending Power*, 148.
49. Hinze, *Comprehending Power*, 148.

understanding of power, we can find a much more constructive view of the relationship between agency and power in the public sphere.

Nevertheless, her advocacy for power-to seems to underestimate injustice, inequality, conflict, and suffering in human life under the oppressive and exploitative structures of power-over, which are intrinsic to all sociopolitical power. I think Arendt's power theory values the process itself of power-to, rather than its results: no matter what some crucial changes in power structure can happen, the process of collaborative efficacy per se can be regarded as power-to. Based on this theory of power, I can presume that the message of power-to can be a powerful resource to reinforce a web of relationships among everyday people so as to act and speak in concert for overcoming a sense of powerlessness. This also offers a great insight into the church's role among everyday people. Even though the church, in a worldly view, may seem powerless or fruitless, the church must continue to act and speak in concert with everyday people, believing that they do generate power by the transforming power of God in this world. Furthermore, her understanding of power-to also sheds a light on the missional agency of US-based Protestant Filipinos who are empowered to act and speak as change agents for the transformation of the Philippines.

Anthony Giddens. Anthony Giddens is a British sociologist, political adviser, and educator and had a great reputation with regard to the theory of structuration and his holistic view of modern societies.[50] In the modern treatment of society and power, Giddens finds a problematic split in the notion of action (freedom) from the notion of structure (domination).[51] Giddens attempts to "integrate two contemporary streams of thought on the subject of power": action theory (from Philosophy) and domination and authority (from social sciences).[52] He argues that structure (domination) both allows and results from human activity (action): "The notion of power and domination are logically associated with the concepts of action and structure as I conceptualized them."[53] In this regard, for Giddens, "Power refers to the range of intervention of which an agent is capable. Power in this broad sense is equivalent to the transformative capacity of human action: the capability of human beings to intervene in a series of events so

---

50. Encyclopedia Britannica, "Anthony Giddens."

51. Giddens, *Profiles and Critiques*, 197–98.

52. Hinze, *Comprehending Power*, 148.

53. Giddens, *Profiles and Critiques*, 197–98.

as to alter their course."[54] In other words, Giddens perceives power as "the origin of all that is liberating and productive in social life as well as all that is repressive and destructive."[55]

Thus, Giddens, unlike other theorists, places a weight upon the integration of action (power-to) and structure (power-over). For Giddens, "power emerges at the intersection between transformative capacity (linked to action and practices) and domination (linked to interaction and structures)."[56] Domination, according to Giddens, occurs when "structured asymmetries of resources are drawn upon and reconstituted in the power relations" that constitute social systems.[57] Thereby, it seems to be necessary that the powerful dominate and the weak are dependent. However, Giddens suggests the term "the dialectic of control" which means "the capability of the weak to turn their weakness against the powerful."[58] In the concept of the dialectic, Giddens accentuates, "all forms of dependence offer some resources whereby those who are subordinate can influence the activities of their supervisors."[59] In this sense, it can be said that everyone still has some measure of power, even when they are oppressed. In Gidden's understanding of power, "Every agent retains some capability of making a knowledgeable difference in a relationship, that is, retains some modicum of power-to or power-over."[60] Therefore, his theory gives a crucial insight that we should not see everyday people with a lower socio-political-economic status as totally powerless, but rather as full of potential. Furthermore, his theory also points out the necessity to address both transformative capacity and domination when one speaks of power, because there is a dynamic interplay between power-to and power-over, which are mutually connected, and eventually engender reality together. Table 2 displays this ambivalent characteristic of Gidden's understanding of power.

54. Giddens, "Remarks on the Theory of Power," 348.

55. Giddens, *Contemporary Critique*, 49.

56. Hinze, *Comprehending Power*, 158.

57. Giddens, *Contemporary Critique*, 50.

58. Giddens, "On the Relation of Sociology to Philosophy," 187.

59. Giddens, *Constitution of Society*, 16.

60. Hinze, *Comprehending Power*, 157.

Table 2. Two Categories of A Sociological Understanding of Power by Christine Hinze

Power as "subordination" (Power-Over)	Power as "effective capacity" (Power-To).
Power's capacity to act *against* or *in spite of* others	Power's efficacy as emerging *with* or *because of* others
Power-over is hierarchical, structured, coercive, asymmetrical and dominating.	Power-to is collaborative and non-hierarchical.
Max Weber, Karl Marx	Michel Foucault, Hannah Arendt,
Anthony Giddens	

Power-over, Power-to, Power-with, and Power-within by Duncan Green[61]

Duncan Green is a developmental theorist currently working at Oxfam (Oxford Committee for Famine Relief) in Great Britain.[62] Green points out the tendency that development policies and practitioners have ignored the deeply unequal power relationships between rich and poor countries when they use the words "partner" and "partnership" in the documents of aid donor and recipient declaration.[63] According to Green, "Understanding power and how it shapes the lives and struggles of both powerful and powerless people is essential in the effort to build the combination of active citizenship and effective states that lies at the heart of development."[64]

Duncan Green's contribution is to diversify the spectrum of power by reflecting the contemporary cases of development, whereas power-over and power-to have been traditionally recognized as two leading forms of power. Green in *From Poverty to Power* segments the concept of power into four:

61. Green, *From Poverty to Power*, 25.

62. Oxfam is a confederation of 20 independent charitable organizations focusing on the alleviation of global poverty, founded in 1942 and led by Oxfam International. It is based in Oxford, England.

63. Green, *From Poverty to Power*, 25.

64. Green, *From Poverty to Power*, 25.

power over, power to, power with, and power within. Table 3 presents the definitions of these concepts. Some parts of power-with and power-within in Green's categorization overlap with the concept of power-to in terms of collaboration and agency. Nevertheless, I think that power-with and power-within have their own significances that indicate a contemporary trend of power in development studies, that is, a rights-based approach.

Table 3. Four Forms of Power by Duncan Green[65]

Power *over*	The power of the strong over the weak. This power is often hidden—for example, what elites manage to keep off the table of political debate.
Power *to*	Meaning the capability to decide actions and carry them out.
Power *with*	Collective power, through organization, solidarity, and joint action.
Power *within*	Personal self-confidence, often linked to culture, religion, or other aspects of collective identity, which influence what thoughts and actions appear legitimate or acceptable.

While Green defines poverty as "a state of relative powerlessness in which people are denied the ability to control crucial aspect of their lives,"[66] he also argues that nobody is entirely powerless and every individual has different forms of power in their multiple relationships. Thereby he accentuates the significance of seeing power in a rights-based approach that "supports poor people to build up their power by addressing both their self-confidence–'power within' and their organization–'power with.'"[67] According to Green, the reason that people have been aware of their rights is that "there have been outside agents such as NGOs, activists, inspirational leaders, academics, or others who have helped to catalyze a process of personal transformation."[68]

The most impressive form in Green's categorization is power-within. Power-within simply means "personal self-confidence." Power is traditionally understood merely "in terms of one person's ability to achieve a desired

65. Green, *From Poverty to Power,* 25.
66. Green, *From Poverty to Power,* 24.
67. Green, *From Poverty to Power,* 25.
68. Green, *From Poverty to Power,* 25.

end, with or without the consent of others."[69] In this format, power ought to prove its efficacy by action or achievement, in which power is often considered as a zero-sum game. However, the concept of power-within argues that everyone has power and has to build it up, without losing others' power for the sake of "my" acquiring power, to a degree to make themselves control crucial aspects of their lives. Moreover, power-within gives rationale to the significant role of culture, religion, and other aspects of collective identity in the discourse of power, as they influence what thoughts and actions appear legitimate or acceptable. Power-within confirms the necessity of this study to explore the issue of powerlessness by not only exterior structural causes (structural evil described in chapter 3) but also interior cosmology (i.e., social imaginary in chapter 4) embedded deeply in culture, religion, value, and identity. In this sense, power-within broadens the spectrum of how to understand and investigate power through the lens of sociology, psychology, and even theology.

Unilateral Power (Power-over) and Relational Power (Power-with) by Robert Linthicum

Robert Linthicum has a background as a pastor actively involved in community development, and a development practitioner of World Vision International. His approach to power is more theological and biblical than that of Hinze and Green. In this regard, the significance of power types by Linthicum is to build bridges between sociological understandings of power and theological one. The way of categorizing power by Linthicum places great weight upon the importance of relational power. According to him, there are two essential types of power: unilateral (power-over) and relational (power-with).[70] Unilateral power has two types of power, that is, dominating power (lowest) and constitutional power (higher); relational power likewise has two types of power, that is, mutual power (negotiating power) and reciprocal power (equally shared power).[71] Table 4 below summarizes his overall concepts on power.

To Linthicum, relational power is "the capacity to organize people and their institutions (churches, social clubs, schools, unions and so on) around common values and relationship so they can act together as one to bring

---

69. Green, *From Poverty to Power*, 25.

70. Linthicum, *Transforming Power*, 81–82.

71. Linthicum, *Transforming Power*, 82.

about the change they desire."[72] However, in the view of Linthicum, there is no power that is originally evil or good. What makes power constructive or destructive is how it is used and for what purpose it is used.[73] Above all, the emphasis on relational power (power-with) is based on a theological understanding of power that reminds us of our relational God and the relational people of God in the Bible, paving the way for an alternative form of power in lieu of the exploitative and oppressive power-over of this world.

Table 4. Types of Power by Robert Linthicum[74]

Unilateral Power (Power-over)		Relational Power (Power-with)	
Dominating Power	Constitutional Power	Mutual Power	Reciprocal Power
The Lowest form, exercised by a government or group through the force of guns and physical intimidation.	A higher or more sophisticated form of power, defined by the law.	Respect each other's influence and position.	The deepest form of relational power. Shared power.
The tyrannical use of power.	Highly structured and hierarchical.	A negotiating exercise of power.	Equally participative in the decision-making, and committed to the common good.
	The kind of power exercised by Pilate in his trial of Jesus.	The power exercised by Jonathan and David in the Bible.	The type of power presented in Deuteronomy.

According to Linthicum, there are two types of relational power: mutual power and reciprocal power. As mutual power respects each other's influence and position, Linthicum explains that it is a negotiating exercise of power.[75] Reciprocal power is "truly shared power in which each party is of equal strength, is equally participative in the decision-making process and is committed not to its private or exclusive good but to the common

72. Linthicum, *Transforming Power*, 81–82.

73. Linthicum, *Transforming Power*, 81–82.

74. Linthicum, *Transforming Power*, 81–82.

75. Linthicum, *Transforming Power*, 82.

good."[76] Furthermore, Linthicum asserts the significance of spiritual power as the "ongoing work of the Holy Spirit in the lives and actions of Christians," which "manifests itself in words, deeds or signs of power."[77] Here is the contribution of his work. The concept of spiritual power offers the groundwork for explaining why the oppressed tend to become the new oppressors once power is gained: "When carried by humanity, relational power can become manipulative and destructive . . . But relational power is never evil or destructive when in the hands of God."[78] Therefore, as Linthicum asserts, "our responsibility as children of God is to use our relational power in ways that please God and transform each other."[79] His theological understanding of power proves why it is so important to think, understand, and live out power theologically.

POWER AND POVERTY

Many social scientist scholars use the word *power* with the definition of *poverty*. The issue of poverty is multi-faceted and too complicated to easily solve. The definition, causes, and solutions to poverty are divergent due to the different views of scholars and development practitioners. Robert Chambers describes the poor as being entangled in "a cluster of disadvantages."[80] According to Chambers, the household is poor because they are entangled in the "poverty trap" resulting in material poverty, physical weakness, isolation, and powerlessness.[81] Interestingly, Chambers points out powerlessness as an invitation to exploitation by the powerful because "the poor fear to offend the patrons on whom they depend."[82] In this sense, poverty is not only a matter of material possessions, but also a matter of power relations in a society. John Friedmann focuses on the powerlessness of the poor and defines poverty as "lack of access to social power," in which Friedmann describes eight dimensions of social power where the poor are unable to move out of poverty and consequently experience "absolute poverty."[83] However, I think his theory needs to be complemented by a theological understanding

76. Linthicum, *Transforming Power*, 82.

77. Linthicum, *Transforming Power*, 82

78. Linthicum, *Transforming Power*, 83.

79. Linthicum, *Transforming Power*, 83.

80. Chambers, *Rural Development*, 103–39.

81. Chambers, *Rural Development*, 103–39.

82. Chambers, *Rural Development*, 133.

83. Friedmann, *Empowerment*, 26–31.

of power because his view on power does not explain why social power and social systems become exploitative to the poor. Tod S. Sloan maintains that the poor speak of psychological dimensions of poverty such as personal powerlessness, voicelessness, shame and humiliation.[84] I think Sloan contributed to the discourse of development in such a way as to appropriate the concept of powerlessness and consequently allowed psychology to join the international conversation of poverty alleviation. Issac Prilleltensky also understands poverty with a focus on the impact of power on individual and communal domains: personal, collective, and relational.[85] Jayakumar Christian describes poverty as "a disempowering system" including a personal, social, cultural and spiritual system in which "the identity of the poor is distorted and remains distorted as a result of a 'web of lies' that entrap the poor in ways far stronger and insidious than physical bonds or material limitations."[86] For Christian, one of the worst lies to the poor is "telling the poor that they are god-forsaken."[87] Ravi Jayakaran understands poverty as "a lack of freedom to grow."[88] Jayakaran depicts the poor as wrapped in a set of restrictions and limitations in four areas of life: physical, mental, social, and spiritual.[89] Thus, the recent emphasis on the use of empowerment for poverty alleviation has resulted in increased attention on the impact of power on individual and communal identity and agency.

The question here is on how power and poverty are interconnected to one another. On the one hand, a socio-economic-political system could be one of the external systems of power that trigger poverty and oppress everyday people in various ways. Edward Royce in *Poverty and Power* maintains, "poverty is caused by circumstances external to the poor–by economic, political, cultural, and social forces beyond the immediate control of the individual." He affirms that poverty originates from "deep-rooted disparities in income, wealth, and power."[90] While his view is relevant to understanding structural causes of power and poverty, this overlooks the fact that the external systems of power are also internalized within the subjectivities of the poor or into their social imaginaries.

84. Sloan, "Poverty and Psychology," 308.

85. Prilleltensky, "Poverty and Power," 19–44.

86. Christian, "Powerlessness of the Poor," 334.

87. Myers, *Walking with the Poor*, 129.

88. Jayakaran, *Participatory Learning and Action*, 14.

89. Jayakaran, *Participatory Learning and Action*, 14.

90. Royce, *Poverty and Power*, 283.

On the other hand, some scholars say that the misuse or abuse of power has deteriorated the reality of poverty. Dewi Hughes pinpoints the interrelatedness between power and poverty. According to him, human power causes or prevents poverty, so that "poverty has to do with the way in which human beings use the power God gave us when he created us."[91] He maintains that the vast number of human beings suffering with extreme poverty is overwhelmingly "the result of the ungodly use of power by other human beings."[92] The word "ungodly" implies a clue that there needs to be a spiritual understanding of power. Bryant Myers also points out that much of what contributes to people being poor has its roots in "asymmetries of power and a resulting misuse of power among individuals, groups, and social systems."[93] However, Myers goes beyond the structural problems of power into the creational and incarnational interpretation of power which provide theological reflections on power, such as all human beings are given power by God; Christians are empowered as human agents by God; how Christians use the power given by God to respond to oppression, and the misuse of power.[94]

Many people, even Christians, tend to think that the word power carries negative connotations, and in many situations these connotations might prove to be correct. History demonstrates tyranny after tyranny by power hungry-leaders bent on forcing their own wills upon society. For this reason, some people, like Karl Marx, think that seeking to abolish such asymmetries through revolution is the ideal. However, James Davison Hunter asserts that "human relations are inherently power relations," and human beings "need each other and the abilities and talents everyone brings to make survival possible."[95] According to Hunter, the imperative for interdependence is the crucial factor to get over "the unequal distribution of gifts and skills" in this world.[96] Hunter affirms, however, that this fact means that "power is inherently asymmetrical . . . . it is impossible to remove oneself from the complex dynamics of power and what power provides."[97] These insights enable us to shift the paradigm in that they exhort everyday

91. Hughes, *Power and Poverty*, 12.
92. Hughes, *Power and Poverty*, 12.
93. Myers, *Walking with the Poor*, 90.
94. Myers, *Walking with the Poor*, 93.
95. Hunter, *To Change the World*, 178.
96. Hunter, *To Change the World*, 178.
97. Hunter, *To Change the World*, 178.

people not to remain in frustration, blaming others for the asymmetrical structure of power, but to move forward to interdependence, understanding and using power that already exists in the structure of a society. Furthermore, to implement social change and maximize the potential of interdependence, Hunter suggests "a theology of faithful witness" by which all Christians "do what we are able, under the sovereignty of God, to shape the patterns of life and work and relationship–that is, the institutions of which our lives are constituted–toward a shalom that seeks the welfare not only of those of the household of God, but of all."[98] Hunter encourages all Christians to become "a faithful witness within" whatever places they may be able to influence and work through networks such as relationships and institutions: the "key actor in history is not the individual genius but rather the networks and the institutions that are created by such networks."[99] For Hunter, cultural change is created by a "practice of faithful presence" that "generates relationships and institutions that are fundamentally covenantal in character, the ends of which are the fostering of meaning, purpose, truth, beauty, belonging, and fairness–not just for Christians but for everyone."[100] Hunter's theory ushers Christians and the Church to recognize the world as the place where kingdom-like transformation should take place, and to strategically utilize all power relations embedded in the networks thereby. In this regard, Hunter's argument aligns with the concept of power-with by Duncan Green, which stands for "collective power, through organization, solidarity, and joint action."[101]

At this point, the insight regarding power by Walter Wink, who is a biblical scholar, theologian, and activist, is germane: "the Powers are good, the Powers are fallen and the Powers will be redeemed."[102] Wink mentions the goodness, depravity, and redemption of power. He gives the reason for abuse and misuse of power in this world. Moreover, the fall of powers causes an impact on both individuals and social systems because people create society and society shapes people. With respect to this, Wink makes a provocative claim, "The gospel is not [just] a message of personal salvation from the world, but a message of a world transfigured, right down to its

---

98. Hunter, *To Change the World*, 254.

99. Hunter, *To Change the World*, 38.

100. Hunter, *To Change the World*, 263.

101. Green, *From Poverty to Power*, 25.

102. Wink, *Engaging the Powers*, 65.

basic structures"[103] Thus, the redemption of power entails the redemption of people, and their social systems as well.

Above all, Wink presents a blueprint regarding how we can bring about the interdependence that Hunter describes. Undoubtedly, interdependence can gain from the redemption of power. Furthermore, the redemption of power could be a key for poverty alleviation. The questions arise: "How can the redemption of power be implemented?" and "What will this look like?" Simply put, "How is the redemption of power rooted in the goodness of power?" In order to answer this question, we need a theology of power.

POWER AND POVERTY IN THE PHILIPPINES

To better understand the characteristics of powerlessness, the words of Walter Wink need to be accentuated as a guideline: "powerlessness is not simply a problem of attitude . . . There are structures—economic, political, religions, and only then psychological—that oppress people and resist all attempts to end their oppression."[104] These sentences precisely describe the major themes of this study in investigating a sense of powerlessness.

A number of scholars, such as Gerard Clarke, Marites Sison, Benedict Anderson, Nathan Gilbert Quimpo, Paul Hutchcroft, Maria Diokno, and Aloysius Cartagenas, attribute poverty in the Philippines to the asymmetric power structure of the Philippines. Generally speaking, there are two culprits triggering the asymmetry of power that perpetuate poverty in the Philippines: patrimonial oligarchy and the extended family system based on a patron-client system.

It has been widely believed that elites of 400 families controlled both the economy and the political process.[105] These Filipino elite families originated from the landowners of the colonial period[106] and constituted a national oligarchy during the late 1980s.[107] Since then, they have been considered the wealthiest and most powerful ruling class in the Philippines, manipulating all the democratic processes and engaging constantly in power games for their own end. In the eyes of these scholars, the ruling elite appears as a selfish, fractious, and greedy group,[108] and ultimately became the major

103. Wink, *Engaging the Powers*, 83.

104. Wink, *Engaging the Powers*, 102.

105. Clarke and Sison, "Voices from the Top," 219.

106. Clarke and Sison, "Voices from the Top," 219.

107. Anderson, "Cacique Democracy," 3–31.

108. Maggay, "Why the Poor," 19; Quimpo, "Oligarchic Patrimonialism," 230.

obstacle to the development of the national economy and politics.[109] As a result, the Philippines has become "a patrimonial oligarchic state," victimized and abused by a powerful oligarchy.[110]

The patrimonial oligarchy enabled a patron-client system, which already existed, to take on a new appearance and then emerge into Filipino history. Because of a patron-client system, Filipino elite families have been able to maintain and even strengthen their own familial ties and hierarchical structures.[111] Consequently, this has been regarded as one of the major hindrances to structural change, equality, and solidarity for the public common good in the Philippines.[112] Some people might argue that these patrons can be good resources for those looking for support. Nevertheless, almost all the scholars mentioned above assert that the patron-client system itself perpetuates the asymmetric power structures and causes a sense of powerlessness of everyday people in the Philippines. In chapter 3, I explain this further with some details from literature and data collected from ethnographic research.

Powerlessness of Filipinos in the Philippines

The issue of powerlessness or helplessness of everyday people with a lower socio-political-economic status in the Philippines is presented by several scholars like David Stravers, Linda Luz Guerrero, and Jose M. de Mesa. In short, according to them, everyday people do not think that they can change and improve their circumstances without outsiders' help[113] so that they are committed to the status quo, and remaining in a sense of powerlessness.[114]

The powerlessness of everyday people is implicit in *Bahala na*, a phrase Filipinos use most often, which is literally translated as "Leave it up to God" or "Come what may." Everyday people say *Bahala na* in a way that seems to hint at fatalistic feelings of hopelessness, when they are confronted with challenging situations and power asymmetries. Jose M. de Mesa affirms that *Bahala na* is "an encompassing concept to characterize the so-called Filipino fatalistic attitude or resigned acceptance of his lot in life."[115] Tereso C. Casiño

---

109. Hutchcroft, *Booty Capitalism*, 53.
110. Hutchcroft, *Booty Capitalism*, 235.
111. Diokno, "Democratising Function," 140.
112. Cartagenas, "Religion and Politics," 857.
113. Guerrero, "Social Inequality."
114. Stravers, "Poverty, Conversion," 334.
115. Casiño, "Mission in the Context," 84.

also points out that *Bahala na* is the Filipino paradigm of folk spiritual-ity (animism, Hindu [AD 900], Muslim [AD 1380], and Catholicism [AD 1500s]) centering on a fatalistic bent.[116] Interestingly, he maintains that "the common practice of combining *Bahala na* (fatalistic worldview) with 'Thy will be done' (faith worldview) produces the Filipino experience of *split-level spirituality*,"[117] which implies that *Bahala na* has religious connotations as well. Ronaldo M. Gripaldo interprets *Bahala na* through the lens of deter-minism which is closely related to fatalism.[118]

Utang na loob is literally translated as "debt of gratitude." This cultural value seems to facilitate interpersonal relationships and a sense of commu-nity among Filipinos. However, the person helped feels obligated to repay the debt in the future, which gives the helper cultural legitimacy to ask the person helped to pay the debt back through whatever possible ways.[119] In this way, the positive meaning of this cultural value can be distorted in a way to manipulate the relationship. As a result, those who are helped and unable to repay the debt feels powerless and many political leaders use these manipula-tive relationships to gain and extend their political influence.

Given the definition of social imaginary by Charles Taylor in *A Secular Age*, the powerlessness of everyday people in the Philippines has become "a sense of the normal expectations" and "the kind of common understand-ing" that enable them "to make up their social life."[120] This hints that the sense of powerlessness functions at the mythic level as some kind of social imaginary. Chapter 4 explains these cultural values causing and perpetuat-ing a sense of powerlessness and examines how a sense of powerlessness can function as a social imaginary in the context of the Philippines.

FILIPINO IMMIGRANTS TO THE USA AND POWERLESSNESS

For investigating powerlessness of Filipino American Protestants, we need to know that: 1) 69 percent of the adult Filipino American population are foreign-born; 2) an estimated 53 percent of the overall Filipino American community are foreign-born, mainly born in the Philippines.[121] There are

116. Casiño, "Mission in the Context," 84.

117. Casiño, "Mission in the Context," 84.

118. Gripaldo, *Filipino Cultural Traits*, 211.

119. Andres, *Dictionary of Filipino Culture and Values*, 190–91.

120. Taylor, *Secular Age*, 172.

121. Cherry, *Faith, Family, and Filipino American Community Life*, 15.

several scholarly writings that deal with the powerlessness of Filipino immigrants in the United Sates. E. J. R. David describes that "many Filipinos in America have extensive experiences of ethnic and cultural oppression stemming from the Philippines and they continue to experience such an oppression in the United States."[122] David also pinpoints that Filipino American adults have higher depression rates than white Americans and the general U.S. population, suggesting that many Filipino Americans may experience psychological distress.[123] Tuason, and et al. maintain that Filipino immigrants in the States experience various kinds of oppressions such as ethnic discrimination, assimilation problems including identity crisis and familial-cultural conflicts that might make them feel powerless in the States.[124] Luis Clement examines relationships between colonial mentality, acculturation, self-esteem, and collective self-esteem with anxiety within the context of the Filipino American experience.[125]

Colonial mentality among Filipino Americans seems to be most closely related to powerlessness. For Filipinos who were colonized during the 1900s by the USA and received the gospel from North American missionaries, the USA was depicted as the Promised Land, the land that flows with milk and honey to prosper the world. Eleazar Fernandez describes the experience from a Filipino context:

> Since colonization entails political and economic control as well as mental control, the coming of Filipinos to the shores of America has been driven not only by the search for "greener pastures," the primary factor, but also by their image of America. For them, America represents the land of endless opportunities and coming to America the fulfillment of that to which they aspire in life. White America represents what is good and beautiful, noble and laudable, while brown Philippines represent what they despise in themselves.[126]

According to David and Okazaki, colonial mentality is defined as "a specific form of internalized oppression that is characterized by a perception of ethnic or cultural inferiority" that "involves an automatic and uncritical rejection of anything Filipino and an automatic and uncritical

---

122. David, "Cultural Mistrust," 59.
123. David, "Cultural Mistrust," 58.
124. Tuason et al., "On Both Sides of the Hyphen," 363.
125. Clement, *Running Head.*
126. Fernandez, "Exodus-toward-Egypt," 170.

preference for anything American."[127] Colonial mentality can be briefly defined as "a form of self-hate in which the oppressed individuals and groups come to believe that they are inferior to those in power."[128]

Thus, powerlessness among Filipino American immigrants might potentially exist in diverse forms such as ethnic discrimination, acculturative stress, identity crisis, familial-cultural conflict, colonial mentality, low self-esteem, and anxiety. Therefore, the powerlessness is not a simple issue defined by one or two main factors but an issue that should be investigated by multi-dimensional approaches.

A THEOLOGY OF POWER

As described above, the redemption of power could be a key toward poverty alleviation. For this, we ought to know how the redemption of power can be implemented and what this will look like. In order to answer this question, we need a theology of power. In this section, a theology of power consists of several biblical-theological themes with a focus on creational and incarnational understanding of power, such as the image of God, the Trinity, Power and Love, Kenosis, and Jesus as the example of exercising power. In addition, a theology of power ultimately centers on the Church as the significant locus where alternative powers should be generated and exercised.

There is no simple correspondence between Christian doctrine and power-over or power-to.[129] Both elements of power are present in Christian conceptions of God, and in the doctrines of creation and redemption. Traditionally, the prevailing power-image of God has been that of omnipotence, with images of God as King, Lord, and Almighty. However, to meet the demands of the times for those who suffer under the asymmetric structure of power characterized by oppressive politics and exploitative economics, it should be the task of missiologists to stress the need for images of holy power as creative capacity, reciprocal and mutual power in addition to the traditional power-over images. Furthermore, we can also think of King and Lord in different ways, that is, beginning with theocracy and then moving on to the power of Jesus Christ.

The basic biblical understanding of power is encapsulated in three ways by Walter Wink: "The Powers are good. The Powers are fallen. The Powers

---

127. David and Okazaki, "Colonial Mentality Scale," 241.

128. David and Okazaki, "Colonial Mentality," 2–3.

129. Hinze, Comprehending Power, 286.

must be redeemed."[130] Wink asserts, "These three must be held together, for each by itself is not only untrue but also downright mischievous."[131] Moreover, according Wink, the powers are not intrinsically evil but only fallen; therefore, "nothing is outside the redemptive care and transforming love of God."[132] Based upon this understanding, various theological concepts with respect to power, such as The Trinity, The Image of God, and The Kenosis of Jesus will be presented in what follows.

The Trinity

The most fundamental concept of a theology of power is the Trinity. Stephen Seamands elucidates that the very names of the three Persons imply existence in relationship: "The Father is identified as Father only by virtue of his relationship to the Son, vice versa. The Spirit is Spirit by virtue of his interaction with the other two. To think of the Trinitarian persons, then, is to think of relations."[133] Colin Gunton echoes these sentiments, noting the relational nature of the Trinity: "God is no more than what Father, Son and Spirit give to and receive from each other in the inseparable communion that is the outcome of their love . . . There is no 'being' of God other than this dynamic of persons in relation."[134] It is remarkable that Gunton presents the word freedom in explaining the relational distinctiveness among the Trinitarian persons. According to him, they "never blend or merge or are subsumed by one another and finally there is freedom in their relations with each other–not freedom from the other persons but freedom for the others."[135] The phrase "freedom for the others" paradoxically shows the uniqueness and distinctiveness of each person in the Trinity. Above all, it should be noticed that freedom *for* others is the outcome of love. This statement gives significant implications on how to exercise power among human relationships in this world, where people seek after "freedom from other people." Jürgen Moltmann contrasts the Trinity as "a community of equals from the Trinity as a hierarchy," by describing the Triune God who "wants human freedom, justifies human freedom and unceasingly makes

---

130. Wink, *Powers That Be*, 31.

131. Wink, *Powers That Be*, 31.

132. Wink, *Powers That Be*, 31.

133. Seamands, *Ministry in the Image of* God, 34.

134. Gunton, *Promise of the Trinity*, 10.

135. Gunton, *Promise of the Trinity*, 11

men and women free for freedom."[136] Michael Downey articulates, "From our origin we are related to others. We are from others, by others, toward others, for others, just as it is in God to exist in the relations of interpersonal love."[137] Mark Shaw describes "four characteristics that define the relationships between the Father, Son, and Holy Spirit: (1) full equality, (2) glad submission, (3) joyful intimacy, and (4) mutual deference."[138] The relationships of the Triune God, thus, teach us how human beings, regardless of the poor, the non-poor, the powerful, and the powerless, should use power for others. In other words, we use our power for others, since this is the way that we have received our being from the Trinity. Moreover, the relationships of the Trinity also alarm those who dominate power and never want to use their power for the freedom for others, and instead exercise power to sustain their societal status and privilege, neglecting the disastrous reality of the powerless.

The Image of God

The image of God or the *imago Dei* is another fundamental concept of a theology of power. It is the relational interpretations of the *imago Dei* that have the connotation of power-with or power-to. Karl Barth has a relational understanding of the *imago Dei* in light of the Trinity: "The relationship between the summoning I in God's being and the summoned divine Thou is reflected both in the relationship of God to the man whom He has created, and also in the relationship between the I and the Thou between male and female, in human existence itself."[139] Simply put, people are created in the image of a relational God.

James D. Hunter states that the *imago Dei* in the creation account in Genesis affirms that human beings, irrespective of socio-economic-political class, who are made in the image of God, "are charged with the task of working in, cultivating, preserving, and protecting creation."[140] Bryant Myers also points out that "carrying God's image empowers all human beings to be able to do the kind of productive and creative work in creation that God wants done."[141] These understandings of power imply

136. Moltmann, *Trinity and the Kingdom*, 218.
137. Downey, *Altogether Gift*, 63.
138. Shaw, *Doing Theology*, 62.
139. Barth, *Church Dogmatics*, 196.
140. Hunter, *To Change the World*, 183.
141. Myers, *Walking with the Poor*, 92.

that all human beings are given a mandate to use the power, given by God, in ways to reflect God's intentions. As Richard Middleton puts it, "The *imago Dei* designates the royal calling of human beings as God's representatives and agents in the world, granted authorized power to share in God's rule or administration of the earth's resources and creatures."[142] This is the functional interpretation of the *imago Dei,* verifying that all human beings, including the poor, the marginalized, and the powerless also, are given power from God. However, this view cannot explain how the power given by God should be properly exercised among human relationships. To some extent, this view may give room for justifying domination over other creatures or even other people, and engendering exploitation. Therefore, we need a better theology that can present power-to, power-with, and power-within, instead of power-over.

Love as the Ultimate Power

In understanding the *imago Dei* and the Trinity as a relational frame, they can be integrated in power and love because the ultimate power is love and love is a truly relational power. Stephen Post affirms, "To be created in God's image means that we are created *for* love *by* love."[143] According to Kierkegaard, when human beings are created in the image of God, "they are supposed to be nothing."[144] Nevertheless, the omnipotent God takes from nothing and says, "Become something even in relation to me."[145] Even though omnipotence does not require anything and a human being is nothing for omnipotence, "the loving God, who in incomprehensible love made you something for him, lovingly requires something of you."[146] Nevertheless, love and power are often contrasted in such a way that "love is identified with a resignation of power, and power with a denial of love."[147] Powerless love and loveless power are contrasted. Even among Christians, we are forced to choose between love and power. When we turn to human affairs, we also may think of love and power as opposed. However, J. Philip Wogaman demonstrates, "In a world of pure, uncontaminated response to God, love would be the only form of power. The power to act would be

142. Middleton, *Liberating Image,* 27.

143. Post, *Unlimited Love,* 20.

144. Kierkegaard, *Christian Discourses,* 127–28.

145. Kierkegaard, *Christian Discourses,* 127–28.

146. Kierkegaard, *Christian Discourses,* 127–28.

147. King, "Where Do We Go From Here?"

exercised only as love, as it is with God."[148] Paul R. Sponheim demonstrates, "the personal, familial and the political must be engaged in any adequate understanding of love," because "love has to do with how people have to do with each other and with how the world runs."[149] Thomas Jay Oord's definition serves us better: "To love is to act intentionally, in sympathetic response to others (including God), to promote overall well-being."[150] However, this does not mean that we cannot have structures and that everyone needs to be on the same level with each other. As Hunter asserts, we cannot live away from the social structures and cannot remove them. Rather, we are called to live in them in such a way as to be aware of the fall and redemption of power and exercise the ultimate power of love in every relationship. Thus, love and power are always together in God.

The Kenosis of Jesus

The kenosis of Jesus showed what real love is and how power should be exercised. In kenosis, Jesus intentionally became a servant, and humbled himself. Jesus could have claimed instant obedience, ordering the apostles to serve him. Instead, he washed their feet and gave his life for them and the whole world. Keith Ward asserts, "Jesus did not take advantage of his superiority over virtually all other humans in status and ability. Instead, he showed what the image of God truly is by serving others, by healing, forgiving, and submitting in love."[151] His self-giving, self-emptiness, and self-limitation through kenosis are the core concepts for explaining what real love is and how power should be utilized. According to Ward, "the lesson of kenosis is a moral one" because it "does not speak of a renunciation of ontological powers, but of a way of exercising those powers in love rather than in pride."[152] This is how Jesus' human life was lived, and it gives a true picture of the nature of the God who seeks to help humans in love rather than dominate them.

Jesus not only taught but also showcased a unique pattern for the utilization of power that stands in stark contrast to the pattern displayed in the world. David Prior draws a clear distinction between two alternative ways of using power: "The first use is the worldly way of exercising power–asserting,

148. Wogaman, "Doctrine of God," 37.
149. Sponheim, *Love's Availing Power*, 8.
150. Oord, *Defining Love*, 15.
151. Ward, "Cosmos and Kenosis," 161.
152. Ward, "Cosmos and Kenosis," 161.

striving, compelling. The second way is the way in which Jesus exercised power, in submission to his heavenly Father."[153] Jesus did not use power in a way to manipulate, but rather "to serve others, not for self-glorification," "to empower others," "to influence, not to coerce," "to promote the freedom to act in accordance with God's will, not to impose God's will," and "to promote collaboration."[154] This sacrificial love can transform the vicious cycle of power dynamics in the Philippines.

THE CHURCH AS THE DIVINE VESSEL OF POWER

Then, how can the love of Jesus be visualized and implemented in the world? This is possible through the Church. Stephen Mott gives steps for social change: "Spontaneous, simple love" toward people in need "grows into a concern for the formal structure of the society" and it "expands from attention to single individuals to the interaction of groups with which the individuals are caught up."[155] Interestingly, Mott also points out "genuine love" that can extrapolate the extent of social action.[156] The church is itself a society. The church is a "purposive social-group" representing the new order that God intends.[157] John H. Yoder demonstrates that "relationships among its members, the ways of dealing with their differences and needs, and the patterns of leadership and decision making constitute a discrete societal structure within the larger society."[158] Thus, the Church can embody the patterns for shared life that God desires for all of human society. In this sense, the Church also can be a sign of the renewal of the human community by the power of God. Therefore, in the words of Mott, the Church is a counter-community: "alternative norms and values are organized into a social grouping."[159] Above all, the power of Jesus as the King of all powers enables the Church to change a society because "He gives the church, by the way of mandate and the manifestation of the Holy Spirit, power to accomplish God's redemptive purposes for the world."[160] The Church is a sign of the

153. Prior, *Jesus Power*, 65.

154. McIntosh, *Paradigm of Power and Authority*, 31.

155. Mott, *Biblical Ethics and Social* Change, 48.

156. Mott, *Biblical Ethics and Social* Change, 48.

157. Dillistone, *Structure of the Divine* Society, 37.

158. Yoder, *Christian Witness to the State*, 17.

159. Mott, *Biblical Ethics and Social* Change, 115.

160. Mott, *Biblical Ethics and Social* Change, 115.

kingdom of God. This is one of the answers to how power can be redeemed and how the redeemed power can bring out social change.

CONCLUSION

This chapter attempted to provide the groundwork for the entire study. I would like to highlight two themes out of many other thematic issues in this review of literature. First, power theories serve as the theoretical tool with which I interpret and analyze the power structure of the Philippines, the power perceptions of everyday people in the Philippines, cultural practices embedded in social imaginaries in the Philippines, and even data collected from my ethnographic researches. In the concept of power-over by Max Weber and Karl Marx, chapters 3 and 4 seek to explore and unveil the structural evil embedded in oppressive politics and exploitative economics. The perspectives of power-to by Michel Foucault, Hannah Arendt, and Anthony Giddens provide everyday people some insightful awareness of the disparity of power structures, causes for powerlessness, and plausible alternative pictures of how to react to these exterior and interior factors causing and perpetuating powerlessness. These power theories provided some blueprints for this entire study for those who feel powerless to overcome powerlessness, and also for those who feel God's call to transform the lives of the powerless. Everyone still has some modicum of power, even when they are oppressed. Therefore, we should not see everyday people as totally powerless, but rather as full of potential (in light of the dialectic control of Giddens and power-within of Green). Moreover, power is not possessed by individuals, but rather, power is everywhere in ubiquitous interactions where people produce knowledge and discourse. For this reason, everyday people have to learn how to release the oppositional power of discourse and knowledge against those of the ruling forces that seem natural for the powerful to use to dominate and exploit the powerless (in light of Foucault). In the same alignment, everyday people should know that power is unleashed when people act and speak in concert (in the view of Arendt), through organization, solidarity, and joint action (Green's power-with).

Second, A Theology of Power is the theoretical groundwork on which this study seeks after the alternative form of power that is biblically based, theologically sound, and culturally appropriate. Alongside Public Theology, A Theology of Power provides the legitimate platform on which Filipino Protestants, both in the Philippines and the USA, should be able to provide, first, an alternative to how power is wielded in the broken world, and then, second, a prophetic voice for those who feel a sense of powerlessness. These would help the ecclesiological role transform the power structures and become the alternative community of love where a theology of power is communicated and practiced. Based upon these sociological-theological understandings of power, this study seeks to present an alternative theological understanding of power through a theology of power, relational power (mutual and reciprocal power by Linthicum), and seven case studies of US-based Filipino Protestants' missional agency (chapter 5).

In the following chapter 3, I investigate structural evil as one of the causes for a sense of powerlessness in the Philippines, with some historical and political backdrops for the contemporary power structures in the Philippines, and more specific and profound engagements in the data collected from interviews to verify my assertion that structural evil is one of the main causes generating and perpetuating a sense of powerlessness in the Philippines.

3

Power and Structural Evil

THIS CHAPTER ANSWERS THE first research question, "How do US-based Filipino Protestants in Texas perceive and understand power structures in the Philippines? What do they think gives power?" Literature on the Philippines and ethnographic research with Filipino American Protestants in Texas discovered that structural evil is one of the major causes triggering and perpetuating the sense of powerlessness of everyday people. This chapter explores the structural evil of the Philippines through integration of the literature on this theme and data collected from my ethnographic research.

Structural evil is referred to the asymmetric structure of socio-political-economic systems that cause and perpetuate a sense of powerlessness. According to my interviewees, everyday people in the Philippines feel powerless because of the malfunction of socio-political-economic structures. Reggie, an interviewee, is one great example for this case, representing how Filipino American Protestants in Texas think about power structures in the Philippines. He states:

> Power structure in the Philippines is the main problem of this country. There have been a lot of studies of why poverty is so rampant in the Philippines. Is it because the people do not know what to do by themselves? You know what? Education is universal in the Philippines. Children have courage to go to school from kindergarten to the graduate school. The reason why poverty is so rampant is because power is controlled by the oligarchs. The "money people" who were raised as powerful controlled everything .... In the Philippines, the poor are very poor, and the rich are very rich.

> There is a very small middle class. Small upper-upper middle class
> and a huge lower-lower class.

According to Reggie, everyday people in the Philippines are very poor
not because of their incapability but the systemic problem of the country,
that is, domination of power by a few elite people on top. In his statement,
power is mostly understood in a form of power-over, that is, oppressive,
exploitative, hierarchical, and coercive.

Structural evil, however, is not a popular topic for Filipino Protestants.
While the Catholic Church has been regarded as a powerful symbol in the
Philippines, one that voices out their official stances on public issues such
as birth control, abortion, and political election, Filipino Protestants tend
to reserve their engagement with public issues. One reason for this is because of their theological propensity. Rev. Collado, an interviewee, demonstrates this case. While studying at a seminary in the Philippines, Collado
worked as a social activist for the urban poor at the grassroots level, trying
to help them achieve their own economic development. Then, because of
this work, he and his team experienced an unexpected response from the
Evangelical Church. Collado states:

> And guess what? Because of our work, we were labeled by the
> Evangelical Church as communists. Organizing the urban poor
> is what the communists do. Right? What Western Protestantism
> came to the Philippines was so conservative. They said, "You
> don't have to deal with it." Something like that . . . So those who
> came to the Philippines were sent and influenced by the con-
> servative denominations who maintain a status quo. So those
> working for the advancement among the powerless people were
> labeled as communists.

Based on the words of Collado, the theological propensity of Evangelical Church in the Philippines has been conservative, which originated
from the conservative theology of American Evangelicals and "inherited
an uneasy dichotomy between private beliefs and public facts."[1] Filipino
Protestants in the Philippines "have not sufficiently explored how power
is used and abused in society and how this relates to the notion of powers and principalities in Scripture."[2] This is the missing part. Therefore,
Filipino Protestants need to be aware of structural evil in society and to
engage in public facts.

1. Offutt et al., *Advocating for Justice*, 15.
2. Offutt et al., *Advocating for Justice*, 15.

To help them do so, this chapter traces back to Pre-Hispanic times and the Spanish colonial rule period in the Filipino history to investigate the foundation of contemporary power structures of the Philippines. Then, we move on to the distinctive traits of power structures in the modern history of the Philippines. In this process, scholarly writings and the data from my ethnographic research will be analytically integrated in a way to explore how structural evil has been situated in the system of the Philippines, and how it might affect a sense of powerlessness of everyday people in the Philippines.

HISTORICAL BACKGROUND OF POWER STRUCTURES IN THE PHILIPPINES

Power Structures in Pre-Hispanic Times

Luis H. Francia in *A History of the Philippines* explains that native societies were made up of three parts: the ruling elite (the *datus* and the *maginoo*),[3] their peers and followers (the *timawa* and *maharlika*), and slaves (the *alipin*).[4] Social relations within the barangay[5] or village were generated and maintained mainly by "kinship ties on both parents' sides and by economic status."[6]

The *datu* was the head of a barangay, "whose authority depends as much on his capabilities in combat, especially in capturing the fled slaves, as on his wealth, the strength and depth of his followers, and his lineage."[7] The *datu* was in charge of determining how to use land and how to tailor barangay economics to meet the needs of the followers through agriculture, fishing, and possible barter with other barangays.[8] Members of a barangay reciprocated by shared labor, such as "helping to harvest his crops, and paying tribute for his household's maintenance."[9]

The middle class consisted of the *timawa* and the *maharlika*. While the *timawa* rendered their services to the *datu* in non-military ways, the

3. The *maginoo* is the class that the *datu* belongs to.

4. Francia, *History of the Philippines,* 31–36.

5. Barangay is a Tagalog word indicating the smallest politico-social unit literally meaning a village, which consisted of thirty to one hundred houses with one hundred to five hundred persons.

6. Francia, *History of the Philippines* 32.

7. Francia, *History of the Philippines,* 33.

8. Francia, *History of the Philippines,* 34.

9. Francia, *History of the Philippines,* 33.

maharlika "functioned roughly as knights did for a king." The *timawa* and *maharlika* "made up his court" and "had a close relationship with the *datu*" in various ways, such as sitting "close by at his feasts", fighting "alongside him in battle", and "acting as his emissaries."[10]

In barangay pre-colonial life, slavery played a crucial role. There were mainly two types of slaves: first, "slaves who were unable to pay back a substantial loan, captured slaves in raiding parties on other barangays,"[11] and second, "the punished slaves for crimes."[12] In general, slaves were considered "a sure sign of one's wealth and status more than land or goods."[13] Nevertheless, social status in native society seemed to be quite malleable. Slaves were allowed to possibly move upward to a higher rank "through reducing one's indebtedness and correspondingly increasing one's social prestige."[14] Thus, status in native society was not determined by the person, but by indebtedness.

Power Dynamics during Spanish Colonial Rule (1521-1898)

In the Spanish expedition to the Philippines, the first key person is Ferdinand Magellan, a Portuguese navigator who first explored the Philippines, which was actually the eastern flank of the Visayas, the archipelago's central region on March 16, 1521.[15] Magellan paved the way for Spain to plant their flag in the Philippines– "a perfect combination of economic enterprise, worldly power, and religious zeal."[16] After the expedition of Magellan to the Philippines, four more expeditions were attempted. The final and most successful expedition was commanded by Miguel López de Legazpi.[17] He initially based himself in Cebu, and strengthened and expanded the Spanish sovereignty to the Manila area in the Northern part of the Philippines by the time he died in 1572.[18] By the beginning of the seventeenth century, the Spanish exercised sovereignty in Luzon

10. Francia, *History of the Philippines*, 33.
11. Francia, *History of the Philippines*, 22.
12. Francia, *History of the Philippines*, 23.
13. Francia, *History of the Philippines*, 22.
14. Francia, *History of the Philippines*, 36.
15. Francia, *History of the Philippines*, 52.
16. Francia, *History of the Philippines*, 51.
17. Francia, *History of the Philippines*, 58.
18. Francia, *History of the Philippines*, 56–59.

(the Northern part), and in much of the Visayas (the Central part).[19] In late 1574, the seagoing Chinese warlord Limahong appeared off Manila, "commanding a flotilla of sixty-two warships, 2,000 warriors, and as many seamen, along with artisans, farmers, and women."[20] By the end of the sixteenth century, as more than 20,000 Chinese resided in Manila and eventually outnumbered the Spanish, the Spanish felt threatened by this rapid growth of the Chinese community. Finally, the extreme tension between them ended with 23,000 Chinese killed.[21] In the late sixteenth century, some Japanese Christians under persecution in Japan "sought and were given asylum in Manila."[22] In summary, the Philippines had been considered "a base for missionary forays to mainland Asia, and by its own ambition of extending its empire throughout the East."[23] Until the eighteenth century, moreover, the Philippines "served mainly as a military outpost, subsidized by grants from Nueva España, or Mexico, the galleon trade, and tribute from the indigenous population."[24]

THE SPANISH RULING CLASS

During Spanish colonial rule (1521-1898), the major figures of power can be simply categorized into three classes: the Spanish Ruling class (the king, the *encomenderos*, friars, *principalia*), the Filipino ruling class (officials), and the local populace (tenant farmers and agricultural laborers).[25] The major reason that the ruling class had power and influence over groups of people was that they controlled access to the land through the system of *encomienda*.[26] In this agrarian social relationship, the tillers of the soil were locked into dependency with landlords. This patron-client relationship in the agrarian system provided the environment for the development of clientelism in politics of the Philippines during the 20th and early 21st century.

Encomendero. The Spanish colony in the Philippines had a controlling mechanism called the *encomienda* ruled by the *encomenderos* who were usually

19. Francia, *A History of the Philippines*, 56–59.
20. Francia, *A History of the Philippines*, 60.
21. Francia, *A History of the Philippines*, 61–62.
22. Francia, *A History of the Philippines*, 62.
23. Francia, *A History of the Philippines*, 62.
24. Francia, *A History of the Philippines*, 62.
25. Francia, *A History of the Philippines*, 64–74.
26. Francia, *A History of the Philippines*, 64–74.

military men who had participated in the conquest and were rewarded with the *encomienda*.[27] Each colonized Filipino was expected to live in the *encomienda* "for purposes of civil government," "for religious instruction," and "for the exaction of tribute and labor."[28] Francia explains this system:

> An encomienda was not a land grant, but rather a system–adapted in all the Spanish colonies–under which an *encomendero* (the term comes from the Spanish *encomendar* or "to entrust") was charged with a number of natives living within a specific geographic area whom he was supposed to instruct in the Catholic faith and the Castilian tongue. Natives living within the *encomienda* were deemed subject to Spanish sovereignty, with the *encomendero* taking on the role of petty king. He had the power to collect tribute, basically a tax, and to expect unpaid labor, or *corvée*, from the inhabitants of the encomienda.[29]

Under the *encomienda* system, the *encomenderos* were a typical figure wielding hierarchical, oppressive, and coercive power over the people. Due to the abuses and cruel exactions from the *encomenderos*, the local populations suffered from poverty and hardships.[30] The friars, who were powerful because of their land and religious privilege, complained of such abuses of the *encomenderos* withholding the friars' fair share of the tributes. For this reason, there was a power struggle between these two power groups, seeking hegemony over the lives of the *encomienda's* inhabitants.[31] Noticeably, the officials in the municipal level were drawn from the *datus*, or the old ruling class of the pre-Hispanic elite. However, the highest position open to Filipinos was at best "that of *gobernadorcillo*, the equivalent of a town mayor."[32] Compared to the malleable mobility of status in native society, the status of native Filipinos during the Spanish colonial rule was obviously limited. Thus, classism had been strictly controlled by ethnicity throughout the history of the Spanish rule period.

Principalia. The *principalia* or noble class were the ruling and educated upper class, comprising the *gobernadorcillo* (a town mayor), and the *cabezas*

27. Francia, *History of the Philippines*, 65.

28. Francia, *History of the Philippines*, 69.

29. Francia, *History of the Philippines*, 65.

30. Francia, *History of the Philippines*, 67.

31. Francia, *History of the Philippines*, 70.

32. Francia, *History of the Philippines*, 68.

de barangay (heads of the barangays) who governed the districts. They "took advantage of the privatization of property, disregarding the tradition of communally held land" by engendering "individual and legal titles to land."[33] As a result, the resident tillers degraded to the status of tenant farmers and agricultural laborers. Moreover, the process of transferring land to the fewer Spanish colonizers grew throughout the 17th century until 1800 so that the provincial hierarchy was made up of "the estate owning friar orders, the land-owning *principalia*, and the local populace."[34] This explains how a small number of elite families have been able to own most of the lands in the Philippines even until today.

POWER AND POLITICS DURING THE 20TH AND EARLY 21ST CENTURY

After announcing independence from Spain on June 12, 1898, the Philippines started the 1899 Philippine-American War, ending in 1902.[35] In the words of Francia, Spanish colonialism was replaced by American imperialism.[36] Filipinos obtained their independence in 1946 after a four-year occupation by the Japanese in World War II and after American rule of about fifty years. To understand power and politics in modern-day Philippines, Ferdinand Marcos should be mentioned. He was president from 1965 to 1986, and ruled as a dictator under martial law from 1972 until 1981. In 1986, Marcos was forced into exile to the United States because of People Power I, a nationwide protest and demonstration against his dictatorship.

Chronological Flows in Viewing Filipino politics

First, Philippine politics can be characterized by clientelism. Clientelism is referred to as "a political or social system based on the relation of client to patron with the client giving political or financial support to a patron (as in the form of votes) in exchange for some special privilege or benefit."[37] The concept of clientelism centers on the domination of power and resources by a small number of people. Clientelist structures, which lasted from the pre-Hispanic and Spanish colonial eras, "began to be

33. Francia, *History of the Philippines*, 72.
34. Francia, *History of the Philippines*, 72–73.
35. Francia, *History of the Philippines*, 144.
36. Francia, *History of the Philippines*, 139.
37. Merriam-Webster, "Clientelism."

incorporated into politics during the early years of American colonial rule of policies, through the introduction of the electoral and party systems on a class based represented by the landlords."[38]

In 1901, during the first municipal elections held as "the initial step towards the building of democratic institutions," the vote was limited to members of the *principalia*, "composed of native local office holders and men of substance in the Spanish colonial administration."[39] Political power was dominated by a small number of people who had been privileged from the Spanish colonial period.

In 1907, the *Nacionalista Party* was founded, followed by the *Liberal Party* in 1946.[40] However, since the very beginning of Filipino parties, their basic structure was determined by the social class of their members because "each party is made up of leaders who bring their respective followers with them, the followers who owe a personal allegiance to the corresponding leaders, not to the party as an organization."[41]

In the 1960s, some Filipino scholars interpreted Filipino politics through the lenses of patron-client relations. Scholars like Carl Landé, Dante Simbulan, and Mary Hollnsteiner described Philippine politics as having been established on the networks of patron-client ties or other personal relationships whereby the elite families extended their political influences by "mutual assistance and loyalty."[42] Carl Landé asserts, "the dyadic ties with significance for Philippine politics are vertical ones, *i.e.* bonds between prosperous patrons and their poor and dependent clients."[43] Dante Simbulan argues that elite families dominated and ran the Philippine political system, using their patron-client connection, wealth, and force to control the country's resources.[44]

In the 1970s, some scholars like Renato Constantino and Alejandro Lichauco asserted that the Filipino elite's power became limited because of America's pervasive influence in Philippine society: "foreign interests actually dominated the country."[45] However, it is unlikely that American's influ-

---

38. Doronila, "Transformation of Patron-Client Relations," 101.

39. Doronila, "Transformation of Patron-Client Relations," 101.

40. Corpuz, *Philippines*, 99.

41. Corpuz, *Philippines*, 99.

42. Landé, *Factions and Parties*; Hollnsteiner, *Dynamics of Power*.

43. Landé, *Factions and Parties*, 1.

44. Simbulan, "Study of the Socio-economic Elite," 1965.

45. Constantino, *Dissent and Counter-consciousness*; Lichauco, *Imperialism in the*

ence diminished Filipino elites' power which had been already embedded in Filipino culture and systems for several centuries. A few years after the fall of Marcos, some other scholars echoed the patron-client framework. John Gershman, Gary Hawes, Walden Bello, and Robert Stauffer maintained that Philippine politics in the post-dictatorship era was returning to "elite democracy of the pre-dictatorship era."[46] Benedict Anderson described it as "cacique democracy."[47]

In 1995, Benedict Kerkvliet reviewed the characteristics and interpretations of Philippine politics and categorized them into three prominent theoretical frameworks: the patron-client factional (pcf), patrimonial or elite democracy, and neocolonial or dependency.[48] In 1998, Paul Hutchcroft described the Philippine state as "a patrimonial oligarchic state."[49] In 1999, John Sidel depicted Philippines politics as "a complex set of predatory mechanisms for the private exploitation and accumulation of the archipelago's human, natural, and monetary resources."[50] These three scholars during the 1990s concurred that a powerful oligarchy had plundered Filipino politics through their strong land-based economic power and their continuing access to the state machinery which became their major means of accumulating wealth.

In the 2000s, according to Nathan Quimpo, the contemporary terminology to describe current politics in the Philippines is "contested democracy," "the combination of the elite democracy interpretation, now the dominant interpretation, with a popular empowerment or democracy from below movement."[51] According to Quimpo, several groups of people like subordinate classes, ethnic communities, and even part of the upper classes compete with the dominant strand of clientelism in Filipino political system, longing for "democracy to mean greater popular participation in decision-making and socio-economic equality."[52] Quimpo depicts the

---

Philippines.

46. Hawes, *Philippine State and the Marcos Regime*; Bello and Gershman, "Democratization and Stabilization in the Philippines," 35–56; Stauffer, "Philippine Democracy," 7–22.

47. Anderson, "Cacique Democracy," 3–31.

48. Kerkvliet, "Toward a More Comprehensive Analysis," 401–19.

49. Hutchcroft, *Booty Capitalism*, 20.

50. Sidel, *Capital, Coercion, and Crime*, 146.

51. Quimpo, "Oligarchic Patrimonialism," 230.

52. Quimpo, "Oligarchic Patrimonialism," 230.

two major competing strands in Philippine politics as follows: "Democracy from below have been somewhat adulterated or deformed by influences of Stalinism and Maoism and also, to some extent, clientelism and populism. Elite democracy and democracy from below are currently the two major competing strands in Philippine politics."[53]

No matter how scholars interpret politics in the Philippines, the bottom line is that the integrating element sustaining all different theories is the patron-client relation and the elite families. In general, these elite families tend to be depicted as the root cause of the oppressive politics, eventually bringing about and perpetuating the structural inequality and injustice of Philippine society.

The Patron-Client Relation

Clientelism has proven to be "resilient and highly adaptable to a range of political, economic, and cultural settings" in the Philippines.[54] Clarke and Sison describe the patron-client relations in a notion on extended families. According to them, Filipinos extend the notion of family "through affinity ties binding people who do not share blood ties."[55] This notion of the family has historically been an important means by which people acquire "patrons who can help them in later life," and equally a means by which "these patrons extend their influence and command the loyalty of wider networks of people beyond their blood relations."[56] Clarke and Sison conclude, "The social roles and characteristics of the family have remained remarkably resilient over time and still permeate business life and politics."[57] The word patron implies "a relationship of dependency that may continue for the lifetimes of those involved."[58] In such cases, the artificial extension of a familial relationship is partly "the result of an inherent economic insecurity that the real family members feel powerless to resolve."[59] In Weber's concept of domination, patrons control the activities of the poor as clients, which means patrons can get the poor to do something that the poor would not otherwise do and the patrons have the power over the poor to produce intended and foreseen

53. Quimpo, "Oligarchic Patrimonialism," 230.
54. Clarke and Sison, "Voices from the Top," 219.
55. Clarke and Sison, "Voices from the Top," 219.
56. Clarke and Sison, "Voices from the Top," 219.
57. Clarke and Sison, "Voices from the Top," 219.
58. Clarke and Sison, "Voices from the Top," 219.
59. Allen, *Psychological Factors in Poverty*, 251.

effects on them. For this reason, everyday Filipinos feel that "income differences between the poor and the elite are too great and experience inequality in which the rich and the powerful get benefited" and everyday people are not "mobilized to change the situation."[60]

Interestingly, Clarke and Sison report that Filipino elites also feel a sense of responsibility towards the poor. The problem, however, is that they want to do their responsibility "on a patron-client basis,"[61] which perpetuates structural asymmetry of power and then persists poverty in the Philippines. The patron-client system in the pre-Hispanic time functioned effectively in a way that "a leader takes care of his followers by providing provision and protection and members of that leader render loyalty and service."[62] However, in modern society, especially in the globalized world, this positive trait of the patron-client system was replaced by "feudal patron-client relationship" whereby "the old sense of obligation towards their own people got eroded and in its place was substituted market contracts for such paternalistic relationships."[63] In the words of Paul Gifford, this "neo-patrimonialism" explains the contemporary trend of more cash-based economics in the political system based on the patron-client relations of developing countries.[64] In this regard, Filipinos attribute poverty to a range of political phenomena including "the inequitable distribution of resources, the prevalence of corruption and the persistence of traditional politics."[65] This suggests that poverty and inequality are widely perceived in the Philippines as the problems of an asymmetry of power.

The Patron-Client Relation and Religion

The patron-client system has been reinforced by religion as well. Paul D. Matheny points out that the patron system in the Philippines is "the product of the domination of religious and political patrons" because it is believed that "the native oligarchy is the result of a native aristocracy formed by the church."[66] As described above in the history of the Spanish rule period, religious leaders have been regarded as the powerful in Filipino

60. Guerrero, "Social Inequality in the Philippines."
61. Clarke and Sison, "Voices from the Top," 237.
62. Gifford, *Christianity, Development, and Modernity*, 20.
63. Gifford, *Christianity, Development, and Modernity*, 20
64. Gifford, *Christianity, Development, and Modernity*, 9.
65. Clarke and Sison, "Voices from the Top," 237.
66. Matheny, "Ferment at the Margins," 202.

society because they have access to the land and have inherited their privilege throughout the generations. Noticeably, several scholars like Paul D. Matheny, and Aloysius L. Cartagenas, have negatively depicted church leaders as a group of elites. This connotes that religious leaders are also the culprits who corrupt society, that they misuse their authority for their own gain and not for the improvement of the lives of the people. Historically, according to Matheny, "at significant moments the ecclesial and social hierarchies have defended the status quo," and "have been identified as arrogant, incompetent, and elitist."[67] Cartagenas asserts that Church leadership (Catholic) in the Philippines has functioned "less as an institution with a moral ascendancy but more as a power broker" by preferring the old framework of church-state relations.[68] In a country where Roman Catholicism is dominant, Cartagenas asserts, church leaders are always tempted to "wear a political garb even as government officials are enticed to constantly seek their blessings."[69] In this way, church leaders "cultivate alliances with the oligarchs, business community, the state and its apparatus."[70] Therefore, the Catholic Church works not "from the logic of empowering poor people but more from the instinct of preserving church interests and a favorable business climate."[71] Thus, Cartagenas concludes, "When the Church fails to provide very moral values and standards in political arenas and cannot effectively function for the common good of society, it falls into being the patrons of the people in the field of religion."[72] As a result, everyday people with a lower socio-political economic status easily become excluded and the patron-client system is reinforced by religion.

Elitism of Filipino Families

People widely believed in the Philippines that "an elite of as few as 400 families controlled both the economy and the political process."[73] Benedict Anderson states that the Filipino elite of the late 1980s constituted "a national oligarchy, composed of the wealthiest and most powerful dynasties," and the Philippines became "a cacique democracy, dominated by landed

67. Matheny, "Ferment at the Margins," 202.
68. Cartagenas, "Religion and Politics," 862.
69. Cartagenas, "Religion and Politics," 862.
70. Cartagenas, "Religion and Politics," 862.
71. Cartagenas, "Religion and Politics," 862.
72. Cartagenas, "Religion and Politics," 862.
73. Clarke and Sison, "Voices from the Top," 219.

political bosses."[74] As explained earlier, the origins of this landed, family-centered elite lie in the pattern of land ownership and control established under Spanish (for 377 years [1521–1898]) and later American (for 48 years [1898–1946]) colonial rule.[75]

During the 18th century, the Chinese mestizo families appeared as the other elite people in the Philippines. The Chinese mestizo families, usually the offspring of a Chinese father and a Filipino mother, began to grow wealthy through certain monopolies in rice trading, and then accumulated massive amounts of land. As a result, they gained prominence for their outstanding socio-economic power among the non-Spanish elite in society.[76]

During 1862 to 1898, in the emergence of a Filipino nation, there were four different elite groups in the Philippines: Spanish mestizos, Chinese mestizos, Creoles (Spaniards born in the Philippines), and the rising native middle and upper classes.[77] Remarkably, for most of the elite families, their ethnicity arose outside of the Philippines.

From the 1900s to 1930s during American rule, the major figures of Filipino political leaders were a Spanish mestizo, Manuel L. Quezon from Tayabas Province (now Quezon), and a Chinese mestizo, Sergio Osmeña from Cebu. This signifies the domination of political power by elite families from a certain of ethnicity at the very beginning of democratic government in the Philippines. In 1907, Quezon and Osmeña easily won the first election in which "the voter base excluded the majority of Filipinos, being limited to those literate either in Spanish or English and with property valued at P500, a substantial sum in those days."[78] In 1935, Quezon and Osmeña became elected as the president and vice president respectively of the Philippine Commonwealth.[79] Thus, ethnicity represented by elite families was one of the most controlling factors to determine classism in Philippine society.

In the post-colonized era, according to Melba Padilla Maggay, the phenomenon of "cultural divide" can be summarized in three categorizations:

74. Anderson, "Cacique Democracy," 3–31.
75. Anderson, "Cacique Democracy," 3–31.
76. Francia, *History of the Philippines*, 110–11.
77. Francia, *History of the Philippines*, 110–11.
78. Francia, *History of the Philippines*, 167; Nowadays the value of P500 is less than $10, but we can presume that it was a great amount of money in 1900s, which the ordinary Filipinos could not afford to have.
79. Francia, *History of the Philippines*, 175.

the elite culture (Spanish-educated *ilustrados* and Americanized techno-crats), the *ladino* (culture broker), and folk culture (everyday people).[80] Maggay explains that during this period of time the elite people were "extraordinarily fractious" from grassroots communities, without sharing "values and a sense of solidarity with the people below."[81] Instead, they were only "in a constant contest for power that has nothing to do with looking after people's interests."[82] In general, the elite families in the Phil-ippines are considered as a group of people mainly who are self-interested, neglecting their responsibilities for the common good in a society. Maria Serena I. Diokno pinpoints the underside of Filipino familism: "In the Fili-pino family, arenas of family (private) interest and public (national) good are highly demarcated . . . hardly any connection is made between family interest and the larger common good."[83]

These extended families are political clans mainly seeking to attain political power by winning elections, to draw more politicians into their political clans, and then to expand their political power and social influ-ence.[84] Since 1987, according to Julio C. Teehankee, "an average of 33.5 per-cent of all lower house representatives elected to the Congress has switched parties in pursuit of resources allocated through clientelistic networks" and "60.2 percent of these party switchers usually jumped into the party of the sitting president thereby producing monolithic political behemoths."[85] Not surprisingly, "57 percent of the legislators from the dominant party belong to political clans."[86] This explains how a small number of elite families have dominated Philippine politics under the past five administrations. There seems to be no ideology associated with politics but clientelism.

Given the propensity of these elite families, they do not seem to be interested in the common good for the anonymous strangers who do not belong to their political clan. For this reason, many Filipinos under the political system of oligarchy think the needs of everyday people are not taken care of by these politicians. Everyday people face inequality, ac-cording to Guerrero, thinking that they cannot organize and mobilize to

80. Maggay, "Why the Poor," 19.
81. Maggay, "Why the Poor," 19.
82. Maggay, "Why the Poor," 19.
83. Diokno, "Democratising Function of Citizenship," 140–41.
84. Teehankee, "Clientelism and Party Politics," 186.
85. Teehankee, "Clientelism and Party Politics," 186.
86. Teehankee, "Clientelism and Party Politics," 187.

change the situation.[87] In sum, Filipinos tend to "attribute their powerless situations to a range of political phenomena" including "the inequitable distribution of resources, the prevalence of corruption and the persistence of traditional politics."[88]

The Ladinos *as culture broker and culture changer*

Exploring the characteristics of power structures in the Philippines, I found, from the article by Melba P. Maggay, the existence of the *ladinos* and their significant role as culture brokers who have tried to bridge these two groups and even brought about some changes in the power structure of the Philippines, like the educated experts who are not from the elite families, but "source their paradigms and tools from outside the indigenous culture."[89] Historically, during the Spanish rule, the *ladino* class was considered "the acculturated group," having the capability to speak both Spanish and Tagalog (native language) for "transacting acculturative collaborations between the Spanish colonizers and native Filipinos."[90] They were not a traditional type of elite people, but had been able to thrive during Spanish colonization because of their privileged status as culture brokers. I concur with S. Lily Mendoza that the *ladinos* possibly participated in the Propaganda Movement to reform abuses and oppression of the Spanish regime.[91] In this regard, the *ladinos* were not only culture brokers, but also culture changers. Mendoza explains,

> The elite have continued to derive from the ranks of *ladino* descent and the European-educated propagandists, with the addition today of Fulbright[92] scholars and other intellectuals sponsored by American foundations, Japan, and other foreign countries. Eventually they also emerged as the elite during the American occupation.[93]

---

87. Guerrero, "Social Inequality in the Philippines."

88. Clarke and Sison, "Voices from the Top," 237.

89. Maggay, "Why the Poor," 19.

90. Mendoza, "Nuancing Anti-Essentialism," 236.

91. Mendoza, "Nuancing Anti-Essentialism," 236.

92. William Fulbright was a United States senator remembered for his creation of grants that fund exchange programs for teachers and students between the United States and other countries (1905–1995).

93. Mendoza, "Nuancing Anti-Essentialism," 236.

As Mendoza states, in contemporary days the *ladinos* as culture brokers were often "co-identical with the economic and political elite but also including middle class intellectuals and technocrats sufficiently educated."[94] Remarkably, the *ladinos'* descendants had moved from the middle class upward to the elite in terms of status. The promotion to the upper class of the *ladinos* in Filipino society brought some changes in power structures. I found a hint from the *ladinos* for my argument that Filipino Americans can be another contemporary form of the *ladinos* potentially impacting Filipino society and making some alternative changes of power structures through their wealth, education, and networks. Chapter 5 discusses this topic with more details.

PERCEPTIONS ON STRUCTURAL EVIL OF FILIPINO AMERICAN PROTESTANTS IN TEXAS

In my ethnographic research, all the informants in Texas were interviewed with some expectations that they would function as a contemporary form of the *ladinos*. Since they were born and raised in the Philippines and then moved to Texas, they could be called "the acculturated group"[95] which sources "their paradigms and tools from outside the indigenous culture."[96] Filipino Americans already had experienced and recognized socio-political-economic structures in the Philippines and continued to be connected with the homeland through familial ties and mass media (SNS, TV, news, internet, and so on). They are able to speak both English and Tagalog. They are well educated and very successful in their professional jobs in the States. Most of all, they are looking forward to seeing a better future for their home country, the Philippines. I believe their perceptions on power structures will be conducive for Filipinos and Filipino Americans to make a difference in terms of how to transform the power structures of the Philippines. In this chapter, I focus on their power perceptions with several sub-themes that can cause and perpetuate the structural evil. Then, in chapter 5, I deal more deeply with this issue through the concept of the missional agency of US-based Filipino Protestants for the transformation in the Philippines.

94. Mendoza, "Nuancing Anti-Essentialism," 236.
95. Maggay, "Why the Poor," 19.
96. Maggay, "Why the Poor," 19.

Power and Political Leaders

This section is to reinforce what I described above with the data collected from my ethnographic interviews. My interviews began with this question: "What is the first impression of power to you?" Interestingly, 95 percent of my respondents answered that power can be both good and bad depending on how it is used. This perception is aligned with that of Linthicum and Wink described in the previous chapter: Power is basically good, but only fallen, and needs to be redeemed.[97] Moreover, my research discovered that especially in the context of the Philippines, power tends to be identified with political power or political leaders who are considered to hold and wield power. For this reason, perception of power by Filipinos is strongly associated with perception of the power holders. If the power holders wield power positively, power is perceived positively. If the power holders do something bad with power, power is considered negative to them. Lyndon, an interviewee, has an example describing in the eyes of Filipino American Protestants how people in the Philippines perceive power associated with political leaders:

> Power itself is neutral. Power can be good if it is used a right way. However, the culture of the Philippines is morally not upright now because of the leadership of the country. I wouldn't say the people in general are not morally upright, but the leadership that's being shown to the people is not morally upright. In the context of the Philippines, power has a pejorative connotation when you use it and people think, "Oh yeah, they [politicians] abuse power." There is a tendency to abuse power on that top level position because they want to hold on to that power. Now power is being used negatively by the politicians and the elite to perpetuate the situation.

It can be said that power is neutral and power can be both good and bad. This statement is ontologically true, but phenomenologically not appropriate in the context of the Philippines because people perceive power through political leaders. For this reason, many people tend to perceive power as something negative through the figures of political leaders. Thus, to explore how people perceive and depict political leaders who are believed to hold and wield power is one of the major keys for investigating power perception of everyday people. Moreover, Lyndon confirms the scholarly opinion that political leaders exercise their political powers and perpetuate the power structures through the patron-client relation and political clans in which they

97. Wink, *Powers That Be*, 31; Linthicum, *Transforming Power*, 82.

have established elite familial ties and expanded their political influence. This is what everyday people in the Philippines empirically recognize. The bottom line is that power per se is perceived as something abusive and negative because of their perception of political leaders in top positions.

Reggie, an interviewee, demonstrates the tendency of Filipinos to associate power with political positions in the government and power is usually viewed as a form of power-over: "But when we talk about power, it is something always associated with the governor, mayor, congressman, president, these people are vested with power. I don't have that power . . . One dominates, one controls, and manipulates. That's the negative sides of power." The interesting thing found in the words of Reggie is that he highlighted that "power in the Philippines is vested in the person" whereas "power in the USA is vested in the institution." This is a difference. This statement explains why Filipinos identify power with political leaders. Patria, an interviewee, also describes power holders as self-interested, not seeking and working for the common good, and noticeably mentions the coercive characteristics of power that can be used to threaten and even kill other people:

> You can determine people with power, especially those sitting in the government. They are the one with the most power over the people . . . . but their power is for their self-interest, not for the good of the country . . . . That's why politicians in the Philippines are really tough. They fight. They could kill . . . . They can just make plans, not for whole country but only for their own interest. And mostly interest will be for wealth, and mostly to be recognized by somebody in the Philippines because they put themselves to be recognized. They want that fear of the people for them.

In addition, Maria, an interviewee, touches on the structural problem of power by mentioning the trait of hereditary politics in the Philippines.

> Like it said, there are a lot of cracks in this system. The traditional politicians have been sitting in the same. And then, the children of the president, there is no end. It's like the vice President, all his families are in the politics. Almost all of them. And then if one retires, the other one will succeed. And then it's like . . . okay, they have the same tactics, and the same hearts. What are they doing for the country?

As demonstrated above, power in the Philippines is usually perceived in the form of power-over, which connotes abusive, oppressive, hierarchical, manipulative, and coercive power. Power or political positions tend to be dominated by a few on top, the elite families, and they are depicted as self-interested groups neglecting their responsibilities for the common good in public spheres in the Philippines. Scholars who have studied the structural problem of the Philippines concur with this assertion that politics in the Philippines has been oppressive and political leaders are the major culprits bringing about and perpetuating structural evil in the Philippines.

Here are the words of Lorenzo, an interviewee, with a more radical voice on this problematic structure of power. Lorenzo stated that the only way to leverage change is to destroy these elites families triggering and per-petuating structural evil. His words intimate how everyday people feel so helpless and powerless because of the structural problem of power:

> You know, when we were talking about this whole Philippine thing with my friend in the States, we feel so helpless, looking at what's happening there in the Philippines . . . . That is so help-less. We came to this conclusion, maybe for the Philippines to move forward again, we have to kill everyone and start afresh. Genocide. Start it over.

I admit that Lorenzo's words are exaggerated and also aligned with Karl Marx's perception on power. Lorenzo obviously represents the sense of powerlessness or helplessness of everyday people because of the structural evil embedded in the entire Philippines. Paradoxically, his statement dem-onstrates how everyday people under the oppressive structure power can be also inclined to think in oppressive and coercive ways. That is because when all other power has been taken away from someone, the person only has coercive power remaining.

Power and Money

Money is considered as another influential factor giving people power. Throughout the interviews, participants were asked about what factor determines who is powerful or what makes people powerful in the Phil-ippines. Their answers fall mainly into two categories: political position and money. Lyndon demonstrates this viewpoint: "When I hear the word power? To me, two things come across. Number one is political power and number two is economic power." Maria pinpointed money as the most influential factor regarding power: "Money. Because only a few people have money, and more people don't have it, the few ones with it can use the money to mobilize the many who don't have money . . . . If people have the money, they will be more confident people, because, like I said, money transfers a lot of things." Maria regards money as something beyond wealth, meaning to say, money can make it possible to force people to do what I want them to do for me, which is reminiscent of the definition of power by Max Weber. Consequently, money gives people confidence, and make people wield their influence upon others. Obviously, money is perceived as a form of power-over.

I was curious which factor is considered more influential between these two, political position or money. On one hand, June, an interviewee, asserted that money itself is more influential than political position especially because poor people in the context of the Philippines are limited in connecting with sponsors and powerful people stick together by themselves. June states:

> I would say in the Philippines it is more of how much money you have. If you have money, you can make things move. When you don't have money, that's when the powerlessness sinks in. It's very hard to move anything, change anything when you don't have money. From what I have seen, power is really based on money because you can get the position you want if you have money . . . The gap between the rich and the poor in the US is not noticeable because most of the people say, "I am a middle class." Even if you don't have money that much, you can be a mayor. You can hold positions in a city. But in the Philippines, without money it is very hard. I think the majority of the powerful congregates together by themselves. It's hard to break into that.

On the other hand, Percival, an interviewee, placed more emphasis on political position than money "because there are people who are not rich and become politicians, and then become powerful . . . .It could be if they have sponsors. Like some big time businessmen, they want to put a person in the position. It can be." I believe this represents a recent change. Money can purchase the status of a patron, whereas in the past it was inherited. Of course, this is plausible only to those who have wealth or those who have social connections with the wealthy, not everyday people with low economic status who are excluded from connecting with the rich. Thus, throughout the entire interviews, one of these two, money or political position, was interchangeably more emphasized than the other, depending on the interviewees.

Power for Poverty Alleviation in the Philippines

I discovered from the interviews that there is a tendency for Filipinos to put a stigma on money, painting the images of political power and money in some negative hues. That is because money in the Philippines is strongly tied with the perception by everyday people of power holders. Reggie, an interviewee, describes the asymmetric structure of power, describing powerful people like oligarchs as "money people," owning and controlling the resources in the Philippines:

> The resources in the Philippines are owned or controlled by 15 percent and 85 percent are the majority who are "under class" or "lower class," very poor people. The power structure in the Philippines is the main problem of this country. There have been a lot of studies of why poverty is so rampant in the Philippines . . . . The "money people" who were raised as powerful controlled everything . . . .They are buying votes.

Reggie points out that many politicians manipulate people by using their money to buy votes, attributing the failure of democracy in the Philippines to the existence of elite oligarchs. His statement represents the point of view of structuralism. In this sense, money is a systemic product controlled by a powerful oligarchy throughout Filipino history. Although this point of view should be complemented by some invisible ideologies beneath the structures, it is true that this view is one of the most popular ways for people to interpret money and power in the Philippines.

Another example linking power with money is given by Lyndon, an interviewee who emphasizes that being promoted to a better economic status is the very way for everyday people to raise their status in society and overcome a sense of powerlessness in the Philippines.

> The main thing right now is money. It's economic power because once you raise the level of the economic status of the people, they can properly ascribe power to the leadership also. Right now, most of the people feel powerless because . . . technically what can they do? They can express their power through political process, through their voting, but most of the time they get it wrong. Why? Because of the education. It's not there. Again, for me it goes deep to see the root of the problem, that is economic situation.

In a deeper level, Lyndon maintains that economic underdevelopment of everyday people is the root cause of political manipulation. Since people cannot afford to pay for schooling, they cannot be educated. As long as they are not well educated, they are not able to discern which candidates are upright or not, just voting for those who bribe them with money. Whereas Hutchcroft in *Booty Capitalism* points out the weakness in political development as the main problem in the Philippines, Lyndon pays more attention to economic disempowerment as the root cause of the structural problem.

Furthermore, Lyndon communicates a significant factor regarding money and power. Money can lift up the status of people and consequently change the power structures of society. According to him, Filipinos working at call centers sourced by international companies for the last ten years are one example of how everyday people can rise in terms of economic status in the Philippines. Nevertheless, he asserts that there should be more systemic improvements empowering everyday people who are economically downtrodden.

> But the problem with economic power is that they are not willing to distribute the wealth. Meaning to say, I am not talking about socialist style of distribution, but just probably more competitive way just for people. I've seen the changes towards for last ten years. That's good. Filipino workers especially in the call centers are getting very competitive raise. But what about the rest of the people are? That economic power needs to be distributed a little bit more . . . . I want a market to dictate that part of the deal. Whatever it's fair, they have to be competitive. There's economic change that will lift up the status of the people. Then, I think, inevitably, power also will be given to them because the people right now are so economically downtrodden. There's no power there . . . giving power to the people is economic empowerment.

I was wondering why Lyndon wants a more competitive market in their economic system. By appearance, the Philippines already adopted democracy as a political system, and a free market as an economic system. Nevertheless, the economic system seemingly does not work for the well-being of everyday people. Hutchcroft has the answer to this in his book *Booty Capitalism*. The capital system prevailing in the Philippines is "rent capitalism" as opposed to "production-oriented capitalism," in which "a powerful oligarchic business class extracts privilege from a largely incoherent bureaucracy."[98] Since it is "rent capitalism" and not "production-oriented capitalism," money has been accumulated through property and land which were dominated and allocated by colonial powers to the powerful

98. Hutchcroft, *Booty Capitalism*, 20.

for more than 400 hundreds years, eventually allowing them to maintain and perpetuate the asymmetric structure of power.

In the same alignment, Lyndon contends that everyday people in the Philippines are economically downtrodden, and remain powerless. In his words, economic development is the way for everyday people to overcome a sense of powerlessness in the Philippines, giving people more power. To verify his assertion, Lyndon presents the case of the middle class in the States: "In the States, the middle class is so powerful because it has a voice, because there is economic power in the middle class. Power is in the middle class because economic power is embedded there. So, they can give power and they can take power." Even though the middle class in the States does not have any political positions except a right to vote, they usually do not communicate a sense of powerlessness. That is mainly because of their economic power. Thus, money is undoubtedly one of the most influential factors in exploring the perception of power by everyday people.

Power and Extraversion

The question that came across my mind was, "Then, why do Filipinos put a stigma on power and money so badly even though everyone is yearning for them?" To answer this question, we need to refer to extraversion. Extraversion is a theory developed by Jean-François Bayart in order to explain a tendency of political leaders in Africa, that is, "mobilizing resources derived from their (possibly unequal) relationship with the external environment."[99] Bayart argues that political leaders in sub-Saharan societies have relied on the strategies of extraversion to "compensate for their difficulties in the autonomization of their power and in intensifying the exploitation of their dependents."[100] In the process of extraversion, those who can obtain relations with external powers, like colonizers, dominate society. As a result, political leaders tend to use their powers to gain major resources from the outsiders mainly for internal political centralization and economic accumulation. Thus, extraversion is a historical product of colonization represented by power-over.

In the history of the Philippines, extraversion featured in a typical form of collaboration with the colonizer, which was criticized by the nationalists during the Japanese occupation and American rule. During the early American colonial period, in the midst of political chaos Filipino politicians

99. Bayart, "Africa in the World," 218.
100. Bayart, "Africa in the World," 219.

were supported by the favorable policy of the colonial government, like "the Philippines for the Filipinos," and "Filipinization," connoting the potentiality of autonomy or even independence and a promise of economic development for the Philippines as long as Filipino political leaders collaborate with the rules set down by the United States.[101] The existence of *Pensionados* is one great example of extraversion. In the early 1900s during American colonization from 1903 to 1912, over 200 boys and girls of the Filipino elites such as wealthy entrepreneurs, and the upper-middle-class families, and the powerful politicians were sent to the States to earn their higher education.[102] In this way, Filipino elites used extraversion to reinforce "class ties between the local elites and their U.S. patrons."[103] Furthermore, there was the assimilation tactic of "fostering a kinship between the new colonizer and the Filipinos," combined with free-trade policies to make Filipinos consumers of American products and make them "become economically dependent on the United States while acting as a source of raw materials and expatriated profits."[104] As a matter of fact, free trade with the U.S. "enabled big business interests in the colony to prosper": "Eighty percent of Philippine export products were meant for the U.S. market. And 65 percent of goods brought in were from the United States."[105] The ruling elites benefited from this strategy of extraversion. Francia states:

> Filipino politicians declared that free trade would hurt the economic interests of the Filipinos, that such a policy favored vested economic interests, opening the country's commerce, industry, and agriculture to domination by American enterprises. In private, the opposition was much more muted, and after intense lobbying, most politicians acquiesced to free-trade policies, in order to protect their careers.[106]

This is a typical example of extraversion, that is, the internal exploitation of power for the accumulation of wealth, consequently resulting in the centralization of their political powers through collaboration with the external power. During Japanese rule in the 1940s, "a significant portion of the elite—fourteen out of twenty-four senators and thirty-five out of

101. Francia, *History of the Philippines*, 166.
102. Francia, *History of the Philippines*, 165.
103. Francia, *History of the Philippines*, 165
104. Francia, *History of the Philippines*, 166.
105. Francia, *History of the Philippines*, 176.
106. Francia, *History of the Philippines*, 176.

ninety eight representatives–collaborated with the Japanese command, to ensure retention of their political and economic power."[107] Collaboration became the politically explosive issue when the Cold War and the threat of Communism emerged in the Philippines.[108] Based on the words of Ramon Diokno, a former chief strategist of Quezon, it appears that Manuel Roxas, the second president of the Philippine Commonwealth in 1946, used the strategy of extraversion:

> The Roxas government, which is headed by collaborators, obviously felt that it could not survive unless it accepted the Trade Act in order to open the way for American financial and military aid. It needed money not only for material rehabilitation, but for the maintenance of an expensive governmental system . . . The Roxas government chose to sacrifice Philippine independence for the sake of the advantage to be gained from American political and military support.[109]

As a result of extraversion, easy access to American products cultivated a preference for such products. Indeed, the term "Stateside" was coined and became popular among Filipinos during that time, implying "a preference for U.S. made products."[110] Public education was implemented in English, which became "the perfect tool for colonial administrators to render identification much easier": "Filipino kids started to dream of snow, yearn for apples, and idolize fair-skinned Hollywood stars."[111] Thus, the process of extraversion made Filipinos more inclined to prefer American products, idolize white skin, pursue speaking English more fluently, and dream of going to the States for a better life. In short, extraversion was used by Filipino elites to benefit themselves, but everyday people from the lower class likewise used it in a way to circumvent the patron-client relationship.

Colorism, preference for a fair skin, is a by-product of colonialism and delivers a symbolic meaning of power. Luz, an interviewee, demonstrates the tendency of Filipino ladies to long for white skin:

> In the Philippines, Filipinos want to have a white complexion and put whitening lotion on the face . . . I even tell my friends here in the States if you see a person on the street walking with

107. Francia, *History of the Philippines*, 181.
108. Francia, *History of the Philippines*, 194.
109. Francia, *History of the Philippines*, 203.
110. Francia, *History of the Philippines*, 177.
111. Francia, *History of the Philippines*, 165.

a parasol, that person is Asian. That is because we're afraid of the sun. We are afraid of being darker. Here in the States, white people use a lot of tanning lotion, but in the Philippines, we have a lot of whitening lotion.

Why are Filipino ladies afraid of being darker? Why do they want to have a fair skin color? What does whiteness mean to them? I argue that their preference for a fair skin is a product of extraversion because colonialism resulted partly in extraversion. Interestingly, according to Maria, an interviewee, skin color and money have strong ties with self-confidence, which is categorized as a form of power-within by Duncan Green.[112] Maria was born into a poor family with dark skin color, which contributed to a sense of low self-confidence in her. In the eyes of Maria, poor people with dark skin in the Philippines tend to be bullied visibly and invisibly. Unfortunately, she was one such case. When I asked her what factors make people powerful or powerless in the Philippines, Maria responded in this way:

> If people have the money, they will be more confident people, because, like I said, money transfers a lot of things. And second thing is, I think, if you look good, it's all like outer appearance, you can get into showbiz. Then you can get into the politics. . . . If you don't have a fair skin, you don't really have the right to show your body. Fair skin, it's the thing. Most of the things in Asian. Colorism. If you are poor and if you are dark, you will not succeed. If you are wealthy and you are white, you will be powerful. Just during my time, but I think it is still true, generally it is . . . . The weak tend to be bullied. And not so good looking cannot really build their confidence, because they are the most bullied people . . . . There is no self-confidence because this is how they grew up. I grew up poor. I had a poor family.

Maria recalled her experience of powerlessness in the Philippines by mentioning three factors: power, money, and skin color. Skin color is not a choice made by individuals. It is inherited from a family. Thus, ethnicity determines classism in the Philippines. In this sense, skin color has a systemic dimension that perpetuates one's identity and well-being in a society. Maria did not have money because she did not have an elite family background. She did not feel she could "get into showbiz" because she had dark skin unlike the elite families of Spanish mestizos, Chinese mestizos, and Creoles (Spaniards born in the Philippines). In the words of Green, her

112. Green, *From Poverty to Power*, 25.

exterior factors like skin color and poverty diminished her self-confidence, and then her lack of power-within influenced her thoughts, actions, and even her self-perception.[113] Of course, there are some other people who persist in the belief that self-confidence originates from interior mentality, which is dealt with in the following chapter 4.

Maria was able to complete her school in the Philippines through financial support from her sister living in the States, and then came to the States to find work. Her sister was part of the third wave of Filipino immigration to the States (from 1965 to 2000), when the United States accepted Filipino skilled professional workers such as doctors, nurses, medical technologist, and teachers, even allowing them to invite their relatives and families. This is how Maria moved to the States. I maintain that the influx of Filipinos to the States needs to be understood in light of a strategy of extraversion between the Philippine government and the United States, even though this is not a typical case of extraversion rendered by the ruling elite class. In the Philippine, as mentioned earlier, everyday people from lower class families have used this strategy as a way to circumvent the patron-client relationship and attain more power-within through outside resources, that is, from the United States, to overcome a sense of powerlessness under the power-over structure in the Philippines.

Furthermore, extraversion provides a new identity. Since Maria moved to the States, she has been very confident of herself as a nurse and excels in her job. According to Maria, she did not imagine that she could excel like this when she was in the Philippines. While pinpointing the structural problem that hinders everyday people from thriving in their lives, Maria's assertion finally came to the zenith through this comment: "Filipinos are smart people. We are smart people. When we leave the country [the Philippines], we excel. But when we are in the country, we cannot excel." Maria has been finding out and establishing her new identity in the States, no longer affected by systemic factors of the Philippines. Her life is a product of extraversion. Her statement not only verifies that structural evil might be a key factor making people powerless, but also signifies how power, especially in the context of the Philippines, needs to be explored in multifaceted dimensions through lenses like money and extraversion.

Many Filipino Americans in Texas are professionals, such as teachers, nurses, doctors, medical workers, managers, accountants, and businessmen. Once they are away from the oppressive structures of politics and economics in the Philippines, many Filipinos have been able to excel

113. Green, *From Poverty to Power,* 25.

among other Americans and prove their intelligence and capability. Filipino Americans in Texas believe that they can improve their situations by their own efforts. It is totally up to them, up to how diligently they work, and up to how effectively they organize their lives. Through this process, Filipino Americans self-construct their identity away from powerlessness and move into a new image of power.

Another factor to see power through the lens of extraversion is language. As mentioned above, the Spanish-speaking *ilustrados* and *ladinos* and later on the English-speaking *ladinos* had power and privilege because of language competency through which colonial powers were able to communicate with the native Filipinos. Especially nowadays in the Philippines, according to my informants, people tend to give more power to those who can speak other languages including English and Spanish. Luz presents this point:

> I would say among poor people, some of them didn't graduate from the school. So they can speak little English. It's hard for them to communicate. Of course, they feel powerless. The person who speaks English well has power. Whatever language he speaks well has more power to him. More controlling, more dominating, something like that.

In this point of view, language demonstrates classism in the Philippines. In addition to this, Percival, an interviewee, presents another interesting point of view regarding language in the Filipino context:

> When people couldn't speak English very fluently or just have a very strong Filipino accent, they have less power. It's a very big thing among Filipinos. When you are able to speak English very well, it affects your confidence. When we speak English, we sound Filipino. For Filipinos, it's a big thing. We are concerned about our accent. We still feel some inferiority complex.

According to this statement, Filipinos both in the Philippines and the States have a tendency not to value English with a Filipino accent. Why do Filipinos feel inferior when they have a Filipino accent in speaking English? Why do Filipinos highly value English with American accents? This phenomenon has a historical root due to extraversion imposing more value on American products than Filipino ones from the time of American colonial rule until now. According to David and Okazaki, colonial mentality is defined as "a specific form of internalized oppression that is characterized by a perception of ethnic or cultural inferiority" that "involves an automatic and uncritical rejection of anything Filipino and an automatic and uncritical preference for anything American."[114] Colonial mentality also can be briefly defined as "a form of self-hate in which the oppressed individuals and groups come to believe that they are inferior to those in power."[115] Colonial mentality can be regarded as one of the negative products of extraversion.

Ironically, the nationalism of Filipino Americans can be used as a strategy of extraversion. When it comes to presidential election, political leaders in the Philippines reinforce political ties with their proponents living in the States. In the case of the 2010 Presidential election in the Philippines, according to Lorenzo, a group of Filipino Americans who fundraised for Benigno Aquino III to be elected as the president of the Philippines was invited to the inauguration ceremony upon his election. Here are the words of Lorenzo:

> There is a group of Filipino Association in the US that helped raise money for his election. After Noy Noy Aquino became elected, this group of Filipinos turned this group into some kind of accountability toward Noy Noy's government. Okay? I got invited to be part of that. During the inauguration of Noy Noy, we all went to Manila for his inauguration, to Malacañang Palace [White House].

Thus, political leaders tend to use the strategy of extraversion to gain and centralize political power with the help of exterior powers like Filipino Americans who have been away from the country, but still maintain their ethnic identity as Filipinos. This hints at structural change in a way that people in the diaspora leverage their power to bring about regime change. Political leaders can use nationalism for gaining political and economic powers because Filipino Americans have a burning desire to fulfill a calling to transform their motherland in better ways. This is a case of extraversion in that "the external environment thus turned into major resources in the process of political centralization and economic accumulation."[116] In this regard, I believe that nationalism of Filipino Americans can be a contemporary resource of extraversion on the side of political leaders in the Philippines.

CONCLUSION

This chapter answers my first research question on how Filipino American Protestants in Texas perceive and understand power structures in the

---

114. David and Okazaki, "Colonial Mentality Scale," 241.

115. David and Okazaki, "Colonial Mentality," 2–3.

116. Bayart, "Africa in the World," 219.

Philippines, and also unveils one cause for the powerlessness of everyday people, with a focus on power and structural evil. From the perspectives of Filipino American Protestants in Texas, everyday people in the Philippines communicate a sense of powerlessness due to the structural evil that is deeply embedded in the form of political power, economic power, and extraversion. As mentioned above, people's perception of power in the Philippines is strongly associated with their perception of political leaders. Since political leaders in the Philippines are notorious for corruption and self-interest, everyday people tend to perceive power in negative hues. Moreover, power has been dominated by a few elite families established since Spanish colonial rule and through American occupation. For this reason, everyday people are limited in their ability to gain political power and wealth. This is how power structures in the Philippines disempower everyday people and perpetuate the disparity of power. Another factor sustaining structural evil is extraversion. Throughout the colonial period and even nowadays, political leaders have tried to compensate for the difficulties in the country with the help of exterior powers like colonizers, and at present the United States. As a result, extraversion brought about colonial mentality, political dependency, and economic exploitation. Concurrently, extraversion is also a tool used by everyday people on the ground to circumvent the powers, and even change the structures.

Power cannot be fully understood from one single perspective. Powerlessness should be investigated in multifaceted angles like politics, economics, ethnicity, classism, and a theory of extraversion. These factors were investigated in light of structural evil as one of the potential causes triggering powerlessness of everyday people in the Philippines. The purpose of chapter 3 was to reveal structural evil in the system in the Philippines, and to help Filipino Protestants be aware of its reality and their role as the agency for transforming structural evil. In addition, I believe that sociological analysis into structures would help them balance their theologies, not limiting the scope of salvation to the spiritual, but rather expanding their perspectives on salvation in holistic ways.

In chapter 4, I discuss another aspect of powerlessness that is triggered by the social imaginary. Since power has multifaceted factors, exploring powerlessness through the social imaginary embedded in people's minds and mentality will expand and complement understanding of this issue.

4

Power and A Social Imaginary

THIS CHAPTER IS MADE up of the answers to the second research question, "What Filipino cultural values or worldviews do US-based Protestant Filipinos in Texas view as causing and perpetuating a sense of powerlessness in the Philippines?" This chapter explores through the eyes of Filipino American Protestants in Texas another factor that causes and perpetuates a sense of powerlessness of everyday people in the Philippines. The issue of powerlessness is too complicated to be defined by one factor. In this chapter, I argue that a sense of powerlessness functions in relation to its underlying social imaginaries in the Philippines. While structural evils were discussed in the previous chapter, this chapter unveils powerlessness by investigating social imaginaries embedded in some Filipino cultural values in which a sense of powerlessness could be implicit. Through my interviews and some scholarly writings, I discovered two Filipino cultural values for the case: *Bahala na* and *Utang na loob*.

To explore whether a sense of powerlessness functions as a social imaginary, I will first introduce definitions of social imaginary by several sociologists and then present how *Bahala na* and *Utang na loob* function as social imaginary causing and perpetuating a sense of powerlessness in the Philippines.

WHAT IS A SOCIAL IMAGINARY?

The social imaginary has been widely discussed in recent years by scholars like Charles Taylor, Benedict Anderson, Arjun Appadurai, and Cornelius

Castoriadis.[1] The topic of social imaginaries ranges "from the capitalist imaginary to the democratic imaginary, from the ecological imaginary to the global imaginary."[2] It is Charles Taylor who is usually credited with the definition of social imaginary. In *Modern Social Imaginaries*, Taylor defines social imaginary as "the ways people imagine their social existence, how they fit together with others, how things go on between them and their fellows, the expectations that are normally met, and the deeper normative notions and images that underlie these expectations."[3] Moreover, social imaginary "incorporates a sense of the normal expectations we have of each other, the kind of common understanding that enables us to carry out the collective practices that make up our social life."[4] In other words, this means a way that everyday people imagine their social surroundings. In a social imaginary people perceive the common understanding, conduct the common practices, and discern a sense of legitimacy. It is through the social imaginary that people have "a sense of how things usually go, of what missteps would invalidate the practices."[5]

A social imaginary is distinguished from a social theory in that "a social imaginary is carried in images, stories and legends rather than theoretical formulations."[6] For this reason, a social imaginary refers to "a culture's wide-angle and deep background of understanding that makes possible common practices, unarticulated understandings and relevant sense-giving features."[7] In this regard, it is appropriate to explore Filipino cultural values in order to unveil social imaginaries.

There are some other definitions of a social imaginary. According to Alberta Arthurs, the social imaginary is "the common understanding that makes social practices both possible and legitimate, which provides the backgrounds that makes sense of any given act in daily life."[8] For Manfred Steger, a social imaginary is a "deep-seated mode of understanding that provides the most general parameters within which people imagine their communal

---

1. Appadurai, *Modernity at Large*; Anderson, *Imagined Communities*; Castoriadis, *Imaginary Institution of Society*; Taylor, *Modern Social Imaginaries*.

2. Adams et al., "Social Imaginaries in Debate," 15.

3. Taylor, *Modern Social Imaginaries*, 23.

4. Taylor, *Modern Social Imaginaries*, 24.

5. Taylor, *Modern Social Imaginaries*, 24.

6. Taylor, *Modern Social Imaginaries*, 23.

7. Taylor, *Secular Age*, 1–2.

8. Arthurs, "Social Imaginaries and Global Realities," 579.

existence," so that it creates "an implicit background that makes possible communal practices and a widely shared sense of their legitimacy."[9] Simply put, a social imaginary provides a platform on which everyday people perceive the common understanding, conduct the common practices, and discern a sense of legitimacy. In what follows, I investigate a sense of powerlessness embedded in cultural values as a form of social imaginary.

SOCIAL IMAGINARIES AND POWERLESSNESS

In the circle of development studies, no one seems to be using the term *social imaginary* in relation to the concept of power. Instead, some scholars mention several different terminologies that designate "mentality and attitude" as one of the main factors that bring about development. Lawrence Harrison uses the term "the creative capacity to imagine and solve the problems"[10] to underscore the role of mentality and attitude in development. According to Harrison, despite the existing structural cracks in a system of society hindering human progress, human beings have achieved tremendous progress throughout history because of creative capacity. In a broad concept, I would say that a social imaginary is partially equivalent to mentality and attitude. Moreover, the term "creative capacity" represents another ramification of power-to, meaning the capability to decide actions and carry them out.[11] Here I see the interrelatedness between social imaginaries and power or powerlessness.

Some similar concepts to social imaginaries are found in the circle of sociology. Max Weber in *Protestant Ethic and the Spirit of Capitalism* stresses that at the root of achievement is a set of values and attitudes that are associated with Protestant ethic: hard work, thrift, honesty, rationality, and austerity–in sum, "asceticism."[12] Weber points out values and attitudes as a determinant to overcoming a sense of powerlessness and bringing about achievement. In *The Sacred Canopy* Peter Berger presents that the religious beliefs and meanings held by individuals construct "plausibility structures" in which members of society legitimate social practices and orders.[13] The contribution of Berger is to pinpoint a significant role of religion in society to form plausibility structures. In the same sense, social imaginaries are

9. Steger, *Rise of the Global Imaginary*, 6.

10. Harrison, *Underdevelopment*, 2.

11. Green, *From Poverty to Power*, 25.

12. Weber, *Protestant Ethic*, 79.

13. Berger, *Sacred Canopy*, 48.

birthed, shaped, and practiced by the influence of religious soil embedded in cultural values. Religion tremendously impacts the formation of social imaginaries and then consequently the mentality and attitude of everyday people, including a sense of powerlessness, because it often uses symbols and other means that tap into the power of imagination. For what follows, I will introduce two cultural practices that connect the psycho-social powerlessness as embedded in Filipino social imaginaries.

Powerlessness and Bahala na *Mentality*

Rolando M. Gripaldo states that *Bahala na* has become "a philosophy of life, a cultural trait that has strongly developed into a significant core of Filipino attitude."[14] Then, the first question is likely to be, "What does *Bahala na* mean? And how do people use this expression in everyday life?" To answer these questions, I need to start with a quote from Teodoro A. Agoncillo's article:

> Can you go through that wall of fire? Bahala na. This is the last morsel we have; where do we get tomorrow's food? Bahala na. Don't gamble your last money: you might go home with pockets inside out. Bahala na. Such fatalism has bred in the Filipino a sense of resignation. He appears indifferent in the face of graft and corruption. He appears impassive in the face of personal misfortune. Yet this "Bahala na" attitude prevents him from being a crackpot.[15]

As the quote above suggests, *Bahala na* is literally translated as "Leave it up to God," "Come what may," "What will be will be," and "I don't care." *Bahala na* is one of the phrases that Filipinos use most often. As a matter of fact, this phrase appears to have "a nationwide linguistic acceptance from more than 80 major languages."[16] Thus, *Bahala na* is widely shared by large groups of people and seems to be the kind of common understanding and normal expectation in which everyday people carry out the collective practices that make up their social life. This fact implies that *Bahala na* functions in relation to a social imaginary.

Despite its popularity, *Bahala na* is an idea that defies definition or explanation because it can be applied in various situations responsibly or

14. Gripaldo, "Bahala na," 194.
15. Agoncillo, "Filipino Traits and Custom."
16. Casiño, "Mission in the Context," 83.

irresponsibly. Nevertheless, many Filipino scholars like Jaime Bulatao,[17] Rolando M. Gripaldo,[18] Tereso C. Casiño, and José M. De Mesa[19] point out the fatalistic attitude that is deeply embedded in *Bahala na*. In everyday life, Filipinos say *Bahala na* when they are confronted with challenging situations and hardships which they are not able to handle and overcome. For this reason, *Bahala na* tends to be recognized as a fatalistic expression. Some other people argue that it can be also used in positive ways as "the spirit to take risks"[20] and "shock absorber"[21] in the midst of insurmountable situations. According to Casiño, "a Filipino toys with fatalism as a means of easing the pain of his or her circumstances, as well as lessening the burden of his existence. In such a case, *Bahala na* functions as a convenient theodicy for Filipinos."[22] De Mesa points out its positive aspect as well: "*Bahala na* provides Filipinos the capacity to laugh at themselves and the situations they are in. It reflects, in addition, the oriental philosophy to be in harmony with nature. While it may appear passive, it is nevertheless dynamic without being coercive."[23]

No matter what its interpretations are, I would like to give an emphasis on the religious connotation deeply embedded in *Bahala na*. I argue that this is not just a cultural expression but also a religious concept even though many Filipinos are ignorant of this. It is important to recognize its religious origin because religion has tremendous impact upon Filipinos' lives. When it comes to ethnic traits of Filipinos, two major things are usually mentioned: trust in God and family-centeredness.[24] Thus, Filipinos are known as one of the most religious peoples in the world. For this reason, it is critical for Filipinos to correctly understand the meanings of *Bahala na* and discern them in such a way as to overcome a sense of powerlessness.

The Religious Origins of Bahala na

Bahala na is rooted in traditional Filipino spirituality in which people believe that "a cosmic force (not necessarily a Supreme Being) controls the

17. Bulatao, "Split-Level Christianity," 119–21.

18. Gripaldo, "Bahala na," 194–211.

19. De Mesa, *And God Said.*

20. Mercado, *Elements of Filipino Philosophy*, 67–92.

21. Casiño, "Mission in the Context," 86.

22. Casiño, "Mission in the Context," 86.

23. De Mesa, *In Solidarity*, 162.

24. Gorospe, "Understanding the Filipino Value System," 65.

flow of the events in the universe."[25] Then, in what kind of religious soil did this expression originate and become rooted in Filipino culture? As some Filipino scholars like Lynn Bostrom and F. Landa Jocano assert, it is believed that "the word *Bahala* was derived from the word *Bathala* in Tagalog that literally means God."[26] In this sense, *Bahala na* reasonably has a religious origin in its usage. Interestingly, Casiño argues that throughout Philippine history, *Bahala na* had been nurtured and established in four different religious soils: animism, Hinduism, Islam, and Catholicism.[27]

The first soil was animism. It may be controversial to state that *Bahala na* originated from animism because there seems to be no strong interrelatedness between animism and *Bahala na*. Ancient Filipinos worshipped celestial beings, nature, and ancestral spirits. Then, how can we relate animism to *Bahala na*? Casiño points out the broad influence of animism manifested even today in the form of Folk Catholicism, and in Philippine society as a whole.[28] In the Filipino psyche, according to him, "the world is a series of karma, an ethical pre-deterministic system of cause-and-effect."[29] Therefore, in this animistic worldview, anything that happens to someone is attributed to a cause, that is, "an impersonal force known as suwerte (luck), tsamba (chance), or kapalaran (destiny)."[30] Casiño tries to explain the ancient spiritual soil for Filipino spirituality. In this sense, the cosmology of Filipinos might function as the essential spiritual soil nurturing the birth of *Bahala na*.

The second religious soil was Hinduism. In the 900s AD, the religious ideas of Hinduism reached the Philippines through Hindu traders from India. A Filipino anthropologist, F. Landa Jocano, asserts that the word *Bahala* originated from the word *Bathala* literally meaning God, but more specifically *Bathala*, known as the highest deity in the folk religion of the Philippines, is of Hindu origin.[31] According to Casiño, Filipinos were able to have the "risk taking and adventuresome trait" because of their faith in *Bathala* who is known as "a powerful yet benevolent deity," consequently believed to "lend, assist, and help regardless of whatever circumstances

25. Casiño, "Mission in the Context," 85.
26. Bostrom, "Filipino *Bahala na*," 401; Jocano, *Folk Christianity*, 5.
27. Casiño, "Mission in the Context," 83.
28. Casiño, "Mission in the Context," 84.
29. Casiño, "Mission in the Context," 84.
30. Casiño, "Mission in the Context," 86.
31. Jocano, *Folk Christianity*, 5.

they have."[32] This interpretation of *Bathala* has greatly influenced Filipino's religiosity in that they not only take a risk in the midst of adversity, but also tend to be fatalistic in waiting for this powerful and benevolent deity. The ambivalence of *Bahala na,* fatalistic and agential, originated from interpreting the meaning of *Bathala,* a Hindu deity.

However, some people might argue that it is problematic to assert a direct cause-and- result relationship between Hinduism and the fatalistic consciousness of ancient Filipinos regardless of the assumption that Hinduism is originally fatalistic. As I explore Filipino history, however, there are some considerable evidences that early Filipino culture with the fatalistic bent of Filipino's religiosity came under the influence of Hinduism in areas such as languages,[33] folklore, arts, and even literature written during pre-colonial period.[34] In effect, religion does not exist by itself. Rather, it is birthed, formed, practiced and melted in cultures, lifestyle, and worldviews of everyday people. Therefore, based on this evidence, I would say that Filipino religiosity had been greatly influenced by Hinduism, particularly its fatalistic bent.

The third religious soil was Islamic faith, which first arrived in 1380 AD through the visit of a Muslim missionary named Mukdum.[35] The Islamic influence upon the fatalistic mentality of Filipinos looks more obvious because of Islam's pre-deterministic consciousness that allows people to "resign themselves to fate (kismet) according to the will of Allah (*Insha'Allah*)."[36] Casiño asserts that *Bahala na* "reinforces the belief that every event and circumstance in the universe emanates from the will of Allah."[37] However, his argument falls into inaccuracy in that he did not distinguish between these two words in Arabic: Tawakkul (توكل) and Tawaakul (تواكل). Tawakkul (توكل) means to reply on Allah and do your best to reach your goal while Tawaakul (تواكل) signifies complete dependence on Allah without making any effort, thinking in a fatalistic way.[38] In the latter, Muslims tend to think

32. Casiño, "Mission in the Context," 84.

33. About 25 percent of the words in many Philippine languages are from Sanskrit and Tamil, which are all of Hindu origin; Postma, "Laguna Copper-Plate Inscription,"183–203.

34. Halili, *Philippine History*, 46–47.

35. Casiño, "Mission in the Context," 84.

36. Casiño, "Mission in the Context," 84

37. Casiño, "Mission in the Context," 84

38. Muslimink, "In Allah We Trust: What *Tawakkul* Really Means."

that if Allah wills, it will happen and no need for any efforts. I think Muslims are expected to believe in the former, but in reality many of them tend to believe and live in the latter. In effect, it is well-known that the pattern of their saying *Insha'Allah* or the will of Allah has a fatalistic connotation. In this sense, I think that Casiño points to the latter when he explains the fatalistic mentality of Filipinos that might have been caused by the Islamic faith. These two different understandings of the will of Allah have greatly influenced Filipino Christians' perceptions of God's will. In sum, animistic religiosity of ancient Filipinos was cultivated in the spiritual soil of fatalistic Hinduism, and then Filipino folk spirituality became more inclined to fatalism under the pre-deterministic attitude of Islam.

The fourth religious soil was Catholic Christianity in the 1500s. When Spanish Catholic friars arrived in the archipelago, they discovered that "Filipinos already had existing religious representations" so that the friars "simply assimilated Filipinos' folk religious expressions in their missionary works."[39] It resulted in "the baptizing of local deities with Christian names."[40] Casiño asserts, "Folk Catholicism developed by giving local deities equivalent functions and powers with patron saints."[41] However, one question arises: "In what specific ways did Spanish Catholicism affect the fatalistic bent of *Bahala na?*" Due to the Spanish friars' strategy of religious assimilation, over the centuries folk religious concepts including *Bahala na* had been accepted without critical objection by Filipino Catholics and then later even many Filipino Protestants.[42] As a result, *Bahala na* seems to be regarded as the equivalent of "Thy will be done" in the Lord's Prayer.[43] Jaime Bulato asserts that this practice of combining *Bahala na* (fatalistic worldview) with "Thy will be done" (faith worldview) have led to the Filipino experience of "split-level spirituality."[44] This syncretistic tendency posed by Bulato and Casiño needs to be further investigated through the eyes of contemporary Filipino Christians through ethnographic research in the Philippines. Interestingly, my interviews with U.S. based Protestant Filipinos in Texas proved that they rarely use *Bahala na* in a fatalistic way, and do not interpret this expression as the equivalent

39. Casiño, "Mission in the Context," 84.
40. Casiño, "Mission in the Context," 84.
41. Casiño, "Mission in the Context," 84.
42. Casiño, "Mission in the Context," 84.
43. Casiño, "Mission in the Context," 84.
44. Bulatao, "Split-Level Christianity," 119–21.

of "Thy will be done." However, my interviewees hinted at the high possibility that this syncretistic tendency could be true in the case of everyday Christians in the Philippines.

Bahala na *as a Product of Filipino Religiosity*

On the basis of these four religious soils mentioned above, the *Bahala na* attitude had been birthed, nurtured, and rooted into Filipinos' mindsets and cultures. Then, another question arises: "Why and how do Filipinos in the Philippines continue to say *Bahala na*?" Casiño has one answer to this:

> *Bahala na* evolves as a religious tool or device in which a Filipino practically copes with the adverse demands and circumstances of life. In order to survive, a Filipino toys with fatalism as a means of erasing the pain of his or her circumstances as well as lessening the burden of his existence. In such case, *Bahala na* functions as a convenient theodicy for Filipinos.[45]

This fascinating interpretation of *Bahala na* in a way pinpoints its religious characteristic. When they say *Bahala na* in adversities and crises, Filipinos tend to be consciously or unconsciously reminded of God or a Supreme Being or a cosmic force or even *suwerte* (luck) or *kapalaran* (destiny), which is believed to "control their lives based on a fixed blueprint."[46] I believe that this religious origin of *Bahala na* enabled it to pass down from generation to generation and take roots in Filipinos' mindsets. Filipinos' religiosity has reinforced this expression to continue to exist and function as a social imaginary. Moreover, as an idea or a story is embedded and passed down in a religious form, a social imaginary is also carried in a similar way to this. Taylor explains this point that social imaginary "is carried in images, stories, and legends."[47] Thus, *Bahala na* is a religious product of different images, stories, and legends of different spiritual soils throughout Filipino history.

Then, if *Bahala na* functions as a social imaginary in the context of the Philippines, in what way is *Bahala na* related to a sense of powerlessness or powerfulness? This question is important because if it is just fatalistic, it feeds upon powerlessness, but if agential, then it is possible to see it as a resource to gain power over a powerless situation. To answer this

45. Casiño, "Mission in the Context," 86.
46. Casiño, "Mission in the Context," 86.
47. Taylor, *Modern Social Imaginaries*, 23.

question, we need to first investigate how Filipinos interpret and practice *Bahala na* in everyday lives.

Bahala na *as a Fatalistic Mentality*

The most popular interpretation of *Bahala na* is to see it as a fatalistic mentality. As mentioned above, this fatalism has been influenced by traditional religious soils. Casiño pinpoints that in daily practice, "*Bahala na* is considered undesirable because Filipinos tend to use it as a negative psychological justification for their failure to take up human responsibility and accountability in times of hardships and crises."[48] According to Casiño, "The downside of *Bahala na* lies in its fatalistic bent where a Filipinos leaves everything up to *kapalaran* (destiny)."[49]

This proves true by the empirical data collected from my ethnographic research. Jerico, an interviewee, states this point:

> *Bahala na* is something like "Who cares about tomorrow?" Let's leave it to luck or destiny. But the word *Bahala* comes from the word *Bathala*, which means God. So the good meaning of *Bahala na* is "leaving it to God. And God will take care of it." But the downside of it is just saying *Bahala na*, meaning to say, leave it to God without doing anything, sitting down, and just leaving it to destiny. So that's also the problem of many people who stay in poverty status. That is a mentality that means "Whatever we do is because we are like this already." They created that mentality that "I'm already this and there's nothing that I can do about it."

Jerico interpreted *Bahala na* as a fatalistic mentality and related it to the issue of poverty. He articulated that people in poverty tend to use this expression in a fatalistic way. This statement alludes that the *Bahala na* attitude might contribute to perpetuating poverty by justifying frustrating situations without doing their best to overcome them.

This fatalistic interpretation of *Bahala na* is supported by another tendency of everyday people, with a lower economic status in the Philippines, to blame the rich and the government for their circumstances. Here are the words of Jerico:

> If you will only depend on the government or other people for your needs, your sustainability will be a problem. You will remain

48. Casiño, "Mission in the Context," 86.
49. Casiño, "Mission in the Context," 86.

in that condition. In the Philippines, we always hear people blaming the rich. They say, "We are like this because of the people who are rich. We are like this because of those politicians who've been corrupt." But, then, my question is, "Have you done something really for yourselves? Aren't you just entertaining that mentality that we are like this and we will remain like this?" I think we have a lot of people in the Philippines who have that kind of mentality.

Thus, *Bahala na* can be used as an expression of the poor people to blame the powerful like the rich and the politicians. As a result, they identify themselves as powerless. *Bahala na* might not represent cosmic fatality, but the fatality of structure. The lack of agency inside people is definitely interrelated to the asymmetric structure of power. Precisely, lack of agency is a by-product of an unjust structure and the structure is reproduced and perpetuated by lack of agency.

In the same alignment, Teresa, an interviewee, explains *Bahala na* in the concept of power-within or personal self-confidence: "*Bahala na* is more of powerlessness. Okay, whatever will be will be. That is when you don't have any power. If you feel like you are powerful, you don't say that. If you are confident, you will do everything that you can do. If you want to give up, you want to say *Bahala na*." To Teresa, those who say *Bahala na* in the midst of challenges and hardships beyond their capability communicate their low power-within or low self-confidence.[50] My ethnographic interviews verify that Protestant Filipinos in the US believe this to be the correct interpretation of *Bahala na*. In other words, only those who recognize agency inside them do not say *Bahala na*. Rather, they take up their responsibility and accountability in times of hardships and crises. In conclusion, *Bahala na* is more used as a fatalistic expression rather than agential, consequently feeding upon the powerlessness of everyday people in the Philippines.

Bahala na *as an Optimistic Spirit*

One lingering question is whether or not *Bahala na* can be used as agential in a certain way. Pe-Pua and Protacio-Marcelino pose an optimistic spirit of *Bahala na*. According to them, *Bahala na* defies definition or explanation because it can be applied variously depending on how one perceives

---

50. Power-within means "personal self-confidence, often linked to culture, religion, or other aspects of collective identity, which influence what thoughts and actions appear legitimate or acceptable." Refer to Green, *From Poverty to Power*, 25.

circumstances, life, power, and even faith in God.[51] As a result, they argue that *Bahala na* is not "fatalism" but "determination and risk-taking."[52] In their points of view, in saying *Bahala na*, Filipinos are "telling themselves that they are ready to face the difficult situation before them, and will do their best to achieve their objectives."[53] In fact, Pe-Pua and Protacio-Marcelino assert that Filipinos are believed to "have probably done their best to prepare for the future situation" even before they have uttered *Bahala na*.[54] This interpretation foregrounds the more agential nature of *Bahala na*, and implies an ongoing process for contemporary Filipino psychologists to re-interpret and re-construct Filipinos' cultural values and ethnic identities.

US-based Protestant Filipinos in Texas are a case for this. They usually do not utter *Bahala na*; the only time they might say *Bahala na* is when they do their best for the good and then wait for God's guidance. Roland pinpoints this:

> My *Bahala na* is, "I'm going to do something good and whatever happens I'm going to stand for it. That's my *Bahala na*. I will leave it to God because I know that God will not leave me. It's going to go through. He's going to help me. If it will fail, I'm still confident because I will get the help of the Lord, because it was just not His will. I guess it is personality and culture. The common *Bahala na* is negative. I don't believe in that *Bahala na*. I believe in *Bahala na* only when it's positive.

Surprisingly, my interviewees in Texas seem to interpret *Bahala na* differently from what everyday people do in the Philippines. As a matter of fact, almost every interviewee answered in such a way that whereas everyday people in the Philippines tend to utter *Bahala na* as a fatalistic mentality, Filipino Americans in Texas tend to use *Bahala na* only in positive ways.

What brought about this difference in its interpretations? What I found from the interview with Roland is that he as a Filipino American Protestant does not believe in destiny, but rather believe in God's will helping those who help themselves. His case demonstrates how theology or faith in God plays a significant role in its interpretation of *Bahala na*. This is aligned with the assertion of Pe-Pua and Protacio-Marcelino, which says that the definition or explanation of *Bahala na* can be applied

51. Pe-Pua and Protacio-Marcelino, "Sikolohiyang Pilipino," 55.
52. Pe-Pua and Protacio-Marcelino, "Sikolohiyang Pilipino," 55.
53. Pe-Pua and Protacio-Marcelino, "Sikolohiyang Pilipino," 55.
54. Pe-Pua and Protacio-Marcelino, "Sikolohiyang Pilipino," 55.

variously depending on how one perceives circumstances, life, power, and even faith in God.[55] For Filipino American Protestants in Texas, *Bahala na* seems to be not "fatalism" but more of "determination and risk-taking."[56] Thus, those in Texas repackage the concept of *Bahala na*, mainly because they theologize its meaning.

How can this same expression as a social imaginary be used and interpreted differently depending on perception of situation, life, power, and faith in God? How should we understand the ambivalence of *Bahala na* in its interpretation and application? To explore the answers of these questions, I found out another aspect of a social imaginary, that is, social imaginary's susceptibility to change.

Susceptibility of Social Imaginary to Change

Noticeably, the social imaginary can change. Jeffery Buckles maintains, "Although the social imaginary explains and reproduces human interaction, it is not static, and is susceptible to change as human knowledge changes, meaning that how humans know, interpret and live in the world is not a constant"[57] Since social imaginaries can change, they "enable humankind to make sense of the world in which they live, as current knowledge is used to interpret the domains."[58] In this regard, *Bahala na* is susceptible to change. That is why there is the ambivalence in interpreting *Bahala na*: a fatalistic mentality and an optimistic spirit. Throughout my ethnographic research, many participants stated that everyday people in the Philippines tend to use *Bahala na* as a fatalistic mentality, whereas Filipino American Protestants in Texas do not. As a matter of fact, almost all my participants answered that they do not say *Bahala na* as a fatalistic mentality, and also have rarely heard this expression among Filipino Americans in Texas. As mentioned, I argue that theology or faith in God played a crucial role in making this difference.

Then, what other factors brought about this difference between Filipinos in the Philippines and Filipino American Protestants in Texas? Based on my ethnographic research, the impacting determinants are social location, education, and time focus.

55. Pe-Pua and Protacio-Marcelino, "Sikolohiyang Pilipino," 55.
56. Pe-Pua and Protacio-Marcelino, "Sikolohiyang Pilipino," 55
57. Buckles, "What are the Educational Implications," 26.
58. Buckles, "What are the Educational Implications," 26.

SOCIAL LOCATION

First, their social location in Texas seems to affect their religious reading of *Bahala na*. Jerico demonstrates:

> I've never heard the word *Bahala na* among Filipino Americans in Texas. Everything is accessible in the US. Those who are not rich also eat what the rich eat here. But you have to work. You have to do something. So, for the Filipinos who migrated in the US, *Bahala na* system does not work. God will help those who help themselves. Manna will not just drop from the heaven. You can always do something to better your life.

According to Jerico, Filipino Americans in Texas seem to not stay in a sense of fatalism. Rather, they appear to believe in God who helps those who help themselves. To them, relying on God does not mean just waiting for God's help without doing anything. Trusting in God requires their responsible actions accordingly. Although theology is still guiding their actions, I would assert that a shift in social location precipitates a shift in theological distinctive.

Nevertheless, I do not believe that all Filipinos in poverty in the Philippines say *Bahala na* in fatalistic ways. I do not also believe that all Filipinos in Texas interpret *Bahala na* with an optimistic spirit. In the words of Buckles, as Filipinos interpret their domains (the Philippines and Texas) in different ways, the interpretation of *Bahala na* changes.[59] On one hand, everyday people under the asymmetric structure of power in the Philippines tend to perceive their frustrating realities in fatalistic ways. On the other hand, Filipinos in Texas believe that they can overcome their circumstances, and everything is possible as long as they work hard in the USA where socio-political-economic structures of power appear to be more supportive to the well-being of everyday people. Thus, the interpretation of *Bahala na* is susceptible to change depending on its social location.

EDUCATION

Second, education plays a crucial role in forming, legitimating, and perpetuating social imaginary by enabling the development of persons. Through education, persons develop a form of consciousness, for "to be conscious of

59. Buckles, "What are the Educational Implications," 26.

things requires some set of concepts through which experience is ordered and made sense of and through this ability to make sense of the world."[60]

The participants in my research evidenced that many of them overcame poverty and a sense of powerlessness through education. The interviewees stated that their continuous education even under the disempowering structures of the Philippines made them self-confident and finally enabled their dreams to come true in the States. Patria, an interviewee, is one example for this case and she states:

> When it comes to low socio-economic status, they just accept that we are poor, and cannot go to school. For me, it is all about my self-goal and self-motivation. My husband and I came from a poor family, not an elite one. My parents were teachers. So they had a little money. But my parents taught us that education is your best tool to improve yourself. We were not trained to depend on the wealth that our parents might have. Not depend on our family. They taught us that you have to desire to be somebody someday. They taught us that we had to study hard, and study well. They told us that once you study hard, you would know how to reach your goal. So it was an individual choice instead of depending on the government or assistance. My husband and I had our goals.

Some people assert that the power structure is the most crucial factor that determines whether people become powerful or powerless. As a matter of fact, many of my interviewees stated that the poor people in the Philippines tend to be fatalistic because of the disempowering structures. However, other people like Patria assert that education motivated her to be successful and organized in her life so that she has been able to develop a form of consciousness. Patria delivered some insights on how people overcome situations and are also overwhelmed by situations. It is dependent upon the mentality of people. In her words, it is an individual choice, and an individual's self-motivation, not structural evil. This connotes how she made a difference by exercising her self-confidence or power-within under the asymmetric power structure where power-over dominates. In the words of Harrison, she maximized her "creative capacity"[61] to imagine a better future, and solve problems she faced. It turned out that the poverty and lack of resources around her life paradoxically reinforced her to keep on seeking self-confidence to improve her life by education. In this sense, it is noticeable

---

60. Pring, *Personal and Social Education*, 12.

61. Harrison, *Underdevelopment*, 2.

that education plays a significant role in awakening people's agency and developing creative capacity of human beings for progress.

In addition, her story also demonstrates how her power-to or self-confidence was wielded to make a decision for her own destiny instead of remaining in powerlessness. In the words of Harrison, power-within and power-to of Patria conquered "a paralyzing and self-defeating mythology"[62] deeply embedded in people's mindsets where powerlessness might take root in. The case of Patria illustrates how education can affect the change of a social imaginary by the intricate interplay between agency and structure.

TIME FOCUS

Third, time focus appears to affect the interpretation of *Bahala na* between Filipinos in the Philippines and Filipino Americans in Texas. Time focus has been one of the significant issues in development studies. Harrison maintains that the worldview's time focus like past, present, or future is of crucial importance for development. He states:

> If a society's major focus is on the past–on the glory of earlier times or in reverence of ancestors–or if it is absorbed with today's problems of survival, the planning, organizing, saving, and investment that are the warp and woof of development are not likely to be encouraged. Orientation toward the future implies the possibility of change and progress.[63]

Harrison points out that more potential for development lies in orientation toward the future, not the past, and today. His assertion hints at why everyday people in the Philippines are more focused on today and tend to interpret *Bahala na* as a fatalistic mentality. June, an interviewee, pinpoints that Filipinos in the Philippines are more focused on present survival.

> They are more focused on surviving on a day-to-day basis. You know, they focus on themselves like "we need to survive." They say, "We need to find a way to get food in our mouth today. I don't care much about what's going on in the local community or in a bigger picture." I think a lot of people in the Philippines are focused on "We need to get through one day at a time." You know, people here in the US have more of the vision for the future. They say, "I can see tomorrow what I want to happen."

---

62. Harrison, *Underdevelopment*, 2.
63. Harrison, *Underdevelopment*, 6.

Power for Poverty Alleviation in the Philippines

In June's view, everyday people in the Philippines might be apt to remain powerless and delay development in their lives because their time focus is on present. That is the reason why they do not plan for the future. Here the new alignment is presented between time focus and plan. The challenges and hardships in their lives might cause people to say *Bahala na* in which they hinder them from dreaming of and planning a better future. This demonstrates how everyday people with a lower socio-political-economic status could become fatalistic.

In the same vein, several interviewees in Texas mentioned the phrase "plan for the future" when they were asked to explain *Bahala na*. It seemed that time and *Bahala na* are interrelated in some ways. Here are the words of Luz: "*Bahala na* is not a good attitude. When you say this, it is because you do not plan ahead of time. If you do not plan, you will fail." Ruth, an interviewee, also states: "People who are not more into planning use this expression. I am more about a planner. You would rarely hear that word from me. I would draft a plan. I am more of an organized person." Patria, an interviewee, asserts: "Bahala na is like whatever comes. No! I don't like whatever comes. I would like to have a plan. I would like to have steps. I write down if I have two things to decide. I write what is good of this and what is bad of that. Then I've never down to *Bahala na*. I plan my life." Interestingly, those in Texas who are focused on planning their future do not say *Bahala na* with a fatalistic mentality. In sum, the different perceptions on time focus of everyday people demonstrates why *Bahala na* as a social imaginary is susceptible to change and why the interpretation of this social imaginary ended up being ambivalent between fatalism and optimism.

Bahala na *and Split-level Christianity*

As discussed above, *Bahala na* has a multi-layered background from different religious traditions. From these religious soils, Filipinos in contemporary Philippine society confront two frameworks for understanding God's will: "either a God who predetermines one's destiny or a God who is interested in and cares for everyday people."[64] In the former, Filipinos "leave themselves to fate" and "simply wait passively on their fortunes or misfortunes."[65] In the latter, Filipinos "live a life of faith, guided in a personal relationship with God."[66] Moreover, Spanish Christianity in the

---

64. Casiño, "Mission in the Context," 86.

65. Casiño, "Mission in the Context," 86.

66. Casiño, "Mission in the Context," 86–87.

Philippines did not transform the traditional fatalistic concept of *Bahala na* to a Christian way of understanding God's will.[67] For this reason, according to Casiño, many contemporary Filipino Christians have tended to "combine faith with fate," and to equate "Thy will be done" and *Bahala na* "without critical reflection and theological objection," which results in a syncretistic form of spirituality.[68]

In my ethnographic research with US-based Protestant Filipinos, almost every participant replied that they neither believe in nor use *Bahala na* in a fatalistic way. As described earlier, the causes for this difference come from various factors such as social location, education, and time focus. Nevertheless, I would like to underscore their faith in interpreting God's will as the major cause of that difference. In the interviews, they communicated an awareness of the agency inside them, which is based on interpreting God's will in such a way that God helps those who help themselves. Their understanding of God's will does not exclude a sense of personal responsibility and of trust in Divine Providence. They showed a good example of how to overcome the syncretistic form of *Bahala na*.

POWER AND *UTANG NA LOOB*

Another Filipino cultural value that potentially causes and perpetuates powerlessness in the Philippines is *Utang na loob*. This expression is literally translated as "debt of gratitude."[69] Every Filipino is expected to possess *Utang na loob*. However, *Utang na loob* like other Filipino values is ambivalent in the sense that it potentially either helps or hinders personal and national development depending on how it is understood and practiced.

Ambivalence of Utang na loob

Utang na loob is, on one hand, basically a good cultural value in the Philippines to practice reciprocity and solidarity. T. D. Andres defines it as "the principle of reciprocity incurred when an individual helps another."[70] Pe-Pua and Protacio-Marcelino assert that *Utang na loob* is "a beautiful element of Filipino interpersonal relationships that binds a person to his

---

67. Casiño, "Mission in the Context," 86.
68. Casiño, "Mission in the Context," 86–87.
69. Kaut, "Utang na loob," 256–72.
70. Andres, *Dictionary of Filipino*, 190–91.

or her home community."[71] According to Mary Hollnsteiner, *Utang na loob* "is designed to achieve security through interdependence."[72] Given that Filipinos are very "sensitive to the quality of interpersonal relationships and are very dependent on them," *Utang na loob* can be used as "a good value facilitating interpersonal solidarity development, and generosity in times of need among the relationships."[73]

In my ethnographic research, Michael, an interviewee, verified its positive aspect: "The positive flipside is that Filipinos are a very loyal people. If you help us once, you can count on our loyalty and friendship forever. To be said of one that "*marunong syang tumanaw ng utang na loob*," which is roughly translated into "he knows how to return a favor," is to be honored highly in our culture." Thus, *Utang na loob* seems to facilitate interpersonal relationships and a sense of community among Filipinos.

However, on the other hand, the problem is the obligation to repay with interest. Since reciprocity is considered an operational principle in Philippine life, "the person helped then feels pressured and obligated to repay the debt in the future in whatever possible ways such as sending gifts or helping the helper in need of aid."[74] Furthermore, nobody knows clearly how much a debt has been paid and consequently "the relationship tends to become permanent."[75] I think part of this reason is due to the high emphasis placed upon relationships. Hollnesteiner demonstrates one example of how and when *Utang na loob* is generated:

> *Utang na loob* reciprocity is created when a person sends a relative's or friend's child through school, paying all or part of the expenses involved. In a period when education is so highly valued as the path to a prestigeful white collar or professional future, the sponsor of these studies creates a lifetime obligation in the child and his family by making possible such a prospect.[76]

Thus, *Utang na loob* is usually created in beneficiary-benefactor relationships among relatives, neighbors, and friends for everyday needs. This shows as well how it is a structural issue. Ruth, an interviewee, illustrates

---

71. Pe-Pua and Protacio-Marcelino, "Sikolohiyang Pilipino," 56.

72. Hollnsteiner, "Reciprocity," 87.

73. Licuanan, "Moral Recovery," 36.

74. Andres, *Dictionary of Filipino*, 190–91.

75. Andres, *Dictionary of Filipino*, 190–91.

76. Hollnsteiner, "Reciprocity," 77–78.

how *Utang na loob* affects the mindset and lifestyle of everyday Filipinos. Here are her words:

> Debt of gratitude is so hard to pay . . . A lot of teachers were telling me, "Why are you still there in a small school?" But I owed the school a lot. That was my debt of gratitude, my *Utang na loob*. So I could not leave them. I've stayed here for twelve years. I don't want them to say, "Oh, you've got your papers done and leave us?" I did most of my work in the sprint like Saturday school, after school, tutoring, and curriculum planning. That was because I owed them a lot. That is how I pay my *Utang na loob*.

Ruth came to the States and became a teacher with the help of one school which petitioned her and provided the papers necessary for her to be a certified teacher in the States. Consequently, she had *Utang na loob* to this school. Ruth is not sure how much of the debt she has paid back. Even when she believes that she has repaid with interest, she cannot be sure the benefactor thinks the same way. For this reason, she cannot leave this school and has overworked for 12 years to pay back her *Utang na loob* to the school. In this way, the relationship between her and the school tends to become permanent.

In addition, *Utang na loob* may pass down from generation to generation through oral tradition in the form of stories regarding the benefactor-beneficiary relationships. Those stories shape the debtors' own life stories and form their image of themselves. As the children of a family grow up listening to the stories about how their parents were helped by someone, they became aware of the benefactor-beneficiary relationships in their family lines. Then the children image themselves based on the stories. This is reminiscent of Taylor's words that social imaginary "is carried in images, stories, and legends."[77]

June, an interviewee, is one such case. She states, "My mom would say something like, "Oh, yes, we have *Utang na loob* to them because when I was applying to come to America they really helped me and pointed me to the right direction. Even if that's 30 years ago, it makes me feel like I still owe that person something, like it's never really paid off my debt." For this reason, the beneficiary feels subordinate to the benefactor. In this asymmetric relationship, *Utang na loob* functions as a social imaginary triggering and perpetuating a sense of powerlessness.

---

77. Taylor, *Modern Social Imaginaries*, 23.

In what follows, I delve into how *Utang na loob* maintains the social hierarchical system in the Philippines, becoming a hindrance to personal and national development. On top of that, I also probe whether it functions for agency or not.

Utang na loob *and the Social System*

Utang na loob as a social manifestation serves as a way to "particularize the functional interrelationship of the upper and lower classes" and consequently "stabilizes the social system," such as the landlord-tenant relationship, the patron-client relationship, the employer-employee relationship, and the powerful-powerless relationships.[78]

If so, how can *Utang na loob* stabilize the social system? In the Philippine cultural value of sharing one's surplus with others, "*Utang na loob* reciprocity is the operating principle which enables a person to lodge a claim on the rich man's wealth."[79] For this reason, those who are in need of help tend to boldly ask for alms from those who have more, even though most of the borrowers cannot afford to repay their debts fully to the lenders. Hollnsteiner states, "this element of insecurity regarding the fulfillment of the debt can maintain the relationship indefinitely and the statuses of the two parties are never equal."[80] In this way, *Utang na loob* generates and stabilizes the superordinate-subordinate relationship between the upper class and lower class. As a result, the disparity of power structures in the Philippines can be fortified by *Utang na loob* so that everyday people with a lower socio-economic-political status might feel a sense of powerlessness.

What then is the psychological mechanism that enables *Utang na loob* to work toward stabilizing the social structure between the upper class and the lower class in the Philippines? It is through *hiya* or shame.

Utang na loob, hiya, *and Power-over*

In the countries like the Philippines where the gap between social classes is wide, *Utang na loob* can be used as a manipulative means for the benefactors to wield power-over beneficiaries and make them remain in a sense of powerlessness. Considering the asymmetric power structures established

---

78. Hollnsteiner, "Reciprocity," 87.

79. Hollnsteiner, "Reciprocity," 87.

80. Hollnsteiner, "Reciprocity," 82.

throughout Spanish colonization and American rule, this cultural value might have been deformed and distorted in ambivalent ways.

Jerico, an interviewee, offers an eye-opening insight to help recognize that *Utang na loob* can operate as a vehicle of power-over,[81] which connotes control and manipulation of other people. He states,

> If I am your manager, and I have given you a decent job, you have *Utang na loob* to me. If I will ask you to do something, sometimes you cannot just say no because of your *Utang na loob* to him. There are always people saying, "You know, that person is helped by him, but he is not returning the favor. *"Walang Utang na loob!"*[82] It can be used as a way of influencing or controlling the person.

Jerico highlights that *Utang na loob* can be negatively used as a way of manipulating or abusing someone. He verifies the ambivalence of *Utang na loob*. How then does it work?

In Philippine culture, *hiya* or shame plays a significant role in practicing *Utang na loob*. Hollnsteiner states, "One should be aware of his or her obligations and repay the helpers in an acceptable manner" like "sporadic services and gifts."[83] Otherwise, the person tends to be considered as "having failed to live up to the standard of the society" and therefore "feels a deep of shame."[84] This person is depicted as *walang hiya* or shameless, which wounds this person seriously.[85] Thus, underpinned by a cultural value called *hiya*, *Utang na loob* functions as a means of rendering conformity to community norms.

In a collective society like the Philippines, being called shameless is regarded as a status lower than a beggar or even a dog. Agaton P. Pal describes this cultural tendency: "A beggar prays for the good health of whoever gives him alms, and a dog barks for his master, but a *way ibalus* (one who has nothing to pay) does not even have a prayer or a bark for his benefactor."[86] In this sense, *walang hiya* (shameless) *or walang Utang na loob* (no debt of gratitude) could be one of the worst insults to Filipinos. Michael, an interviewee,

---

81. According to Hinze, Max Weber's theory is categorized as power-over, which is hierarchical, structured, coercive, asymmetrical and dominating. Refer to: Hinze, *Comprehending Power in Christian Social Ethics*, 5.

82. Literally this means, "Don't you have a debt of gratitude?"

83. Hollnsteiner, "Reciprocity," 74.

84. Hollnsteiner, "Reciprocity," 74–75.

85. Hollnsteiner, "Reciprocity," 74–75.

86. Pal, "Philippine Barrio," 333–486.

verifies this point: "It is easily perverted because it is more dishonorable to be perceived as ungrateful than to be corrupt or unjust." Therefore, to avoid being called *walang utang na loob,* or lacking a debt of gratitude, beneficiaries tend to obey whatever benefactors ask them to do even though they may not want to do it. Interestingly, this is a typical description of power-over. Reggie, an interviewee, supports this point of view:

> When someone helps you in the Philippines, you express a debt of gratitude at a certain point. You cannot even attack or criticize the person. Why? They say, "You don't have *Utang na loob?*" They use it as a weapon against you. They will say, "Hey, I will help this person. He is not going to do anything against me. He will not say anything against me. He will not squeal on me. He will not say about me in the public because of a debt of gratitude.

Reggie points to the propensity of some people to intentionally put *Utang na loob* on other people for personal purposes. Luz, an interviewee, demonstrates this asymmetric relationship between two parties in terms of destiny: "If you feel like you keep on paying *Utang na loob,* you will be in total debt. You can never repay the person fully. It's like he is holding your destiny in his hands." Thus, *Utang na loob* is used to control people's behavior, decision, and even destiny, which connotes manifestations of power-over based on the definition of Max Weber and Duncan Green.[87]

Utang na loob *and Corruption*

Considering the definitions of a social imaginary, *Utang na loob* shows a great deal of Filipino social imaginary because *Utang na loob* "incorporates a sense of the normal expectations" Filipinos have of each other, and "the kind of common understanding" that enables them to carry out "the collective practices that make up our social life."[88] Consequently, *Utang na loob* as a social imaginary permeates and influences all facets of the Filipino way of life: business, education, politics, morality and religion. However, according to Jaime Bulatao, *Utang na loob* has been blamed for "almost all the evils of Philippine society such as the lagay system (bribery

---

87. Power-over means, "The power of the strong over the weak. This power is often hidden – for example, what elites manage to keep off the table of political debate." Refer to: Duncan Green, *From Poverty to Power,* 25.

88. Taylor, *Modern Social Imaginaries,* 24.

and extortion), graft and corruption in politics and in the government, smuggling, and so forth."[89]

My ethnographic research proves this true. The worst downside of *Utang na loob* is manifested when it is used by politicians to buy votes in an election, and for Filipino voters to be willing to sell their votes in order to return a favor done for them by politicians. One of my interviewees exemplifies how politicians can buy votes during the election:

> Every election they [politicians] will distribute envelopes with money to every voter in the voting places. People just line up and get their money, and go vote . . . This is why the Philippines is not changing. We are selling our votes . . . They just turn a blind eye. They receive money. If we really need to change the system in the Philippines, we need to change ourselves. We should not be selling our votes so we can elect the right serving politicians. Politicians who buy your votes will get back that money by corrupting whatever budgets from the government.

As a matter of fact, many politicians in the Philippines intentionally use *Utang na loob* with people by giving them handouts or money in order to ask people to vote for them. Political leaders, cognizant of the social system, exploit it by deliberately cultivating *Utang na loob* debts so that when voting time comes, they can reclaim these by requesting the debtors to vote for them or for their candidate. This behavior of cultivating *Utang na loob* debt is sourced from a social imaginary and has become a sense of the normal expectation, a kind of common understanding, and a collective practice in the entire nation of the Philippines.

Here is another example of this from my research. One interviewee describes how a mayor of Makati City in Manila used debt of gratitude with everyday people:

> He just gave people a piece of meals in order to look good. Then, after a while, he gave clothing to the kids, maybe three T-shirts for each kid. So he would think, "I look good." So if I am the person receiving something from him, all I am expecting is that the mayor will give me something again . . . So what he was doing is just helping them little by little so that people would keep asking and depending on him instead of improving their lives as a whole . . . You know, they are just like chickens that he feeds. That is the wrong way to help people . . . So every election, of course, he wins because this is the way he trains and manipulates people.

89. Bulatao, *Split-Level Christianity,* 44.

Although the voters are aware of their agency, power-to,[90] in the words of Foucault they did not release "the oppositional power of discourse and knowledge that the ruling forces have submerged."[91] For Foucault, opposition voices are a vehicle for altering that power. Although the candidate does not deserve their votes, in general, the debtors' sense of honor and propriety force them to comply regardless of the quality of the candidate involved. In this case, those who have a larger group of *Utang na loob* debtors tend to win the elections. Thus, *Utang na loob* is deeply embedded in the mindset of Filipinos, and became an operational principle of everyday life in the Philippines. In this way, politicians wield power over everyday people through *Utang na loob* and everyday people fail to exercise their power-to for alternative actions and carrying them out.[92]

Lyndon, an interviewee, regards cronyism and nepotism as other forms of corruption, which usually result from *Utang na looob*. According to Lyndon, cronyism through *Utang na loob* is endemic in politics especially between the businessmen and political parties. He states,

> For example, if I have a million pesos to invest in your political campaign, I will give it to you with expecting a position in the government. By virtue of *Utang na loob,* you will honor that value . . . There are 24 Senators in the Philippines. If you get picked by the party, you will get voted in. If you are elected, that will become your *Utang na loob* which goes with the party, party's wishes, party's direction. Whatever the political party says to you, you have to follow it. You become a "yes man" because you are indebted.

In his interview, "A yes man" signifies the negative aspect of *Utang na loob* in the sense that one who is beholden to another person will do anything to please him, thinking that by doing so he is able to repay a debt. For this reason, one condones what the other person does and will never censure him for wrongdoing. In this way, *Utang na loob* functions as a social imaginary, granting an indulgence to corruption in the Philippines.

---

90. According to Hinze, Power-to can be defined as "effective capacity," which means "primarily people's ability to affect their ends." Power-to is collaborative and non-hierarchical. Refer to: Hinze, *Comprehending Power*, 5.

91. Hinze, *Comprehending Power*, 123.

92. According to Green, power-to is defined as "the capability to decide actions and carry them out"; Refer to: Green, *From Poverty to Power*, 25.

Utang na loob *and Social Change*

Utang na loob is basically known as a good cultural value in the Philippines to practice reciprocity and solidarity. However, my interviews show that *Utang na loob* functions as a social imaginary to stabilize the disparity of power structure through the *hiya* or *shame* concept. This case demonstrates how a good cultural value can be distorted in a way that sustains the unjust power structure. One participant in my research, Michael, offers a good summary: "On a personal-relationship basis, it is used more positively. But in more systemic situations (government, business, etc.), it turns to be more negative." This statement brings about another question: "Why did this good value end up functioning negatively in a system? What is the mechanism to render this possible?"

Linthicum offers a hint to this question. He asserts, "Structures are necessary for the values to be practiced effectively."[93] According to him, there are two types of values: articulated and unarticulated. Articulated values are "those to which the populace of a system gives clear recognition."[94] For example, most everyday people in the Philippines recognize that *Utang na loob* is a good cultural value providing reciprocity and solidarity. On the contrary, the unarticulated values are "those beliefs and convictions that are rarely given voice but serve as operating assumptions for those who hold considerable power in the system."[95] For example, everyday people are aware of the downside of *Utang na loob*, but do not articulate it in public. However, they still practice it under tacit agreement. Therefore, the negative side of *Utang na loob* functions as an unarticulated value in the system of Filipino societies. As Linthicum pinpoints, unarticulated values are usually more powerful than the articulated values.[96] The "articulated values" like "Do not sell our votes due to *Utang na loob*" are not lived out well. Rather, the "unarticulated values" like "I want to pay him back by selling my vote no matter whether the candidate is qualified for this position" works out more powerfully than the former. Therefore, regardless of its merits, *Utang na loob* is controlled, dominated, and even distorted by those who hold power-over. This explains why a good cultural value sustains the unjust power structure, and how a good cultural value turns into a negative one under the corrupt

93. Linthicum, *Transforming Power*, 25.
94. Linthicum, *Transforming Power*, 25.
95. Linthicum, *Transforming Power*, 25.
96. Linthicum, *Transforming Power*, 25.

system. That is why we have to seek after transforming both the individuals' mindsets and social structures at the same time.

In my research, I was curious about how US-based Filipino Protestants understand and practice *Utang na loob* and how *Utang na loob* influences relationships in the church. To my surprise, almost all of them answered similarly that they do not practice and experience *Utang na loob* in the church. In addition, they mentioned that many Filipino Americans in the community carried *Utang na loob* to the States and still practice it among Filipinos. Then, why is *Utang na loob* rarely practiced in the church? What brought about this difference? Reggie, one of the participants in the ethnographic research, provides an incredible reason:

> That is because we believe in the Gospel of Jesus Christ. Now we are supposed to be a new person. That's why Paul says in 2 Corinthians 5:17, "Therefore, you are now a new creation. The old passed away." I am still aware of these cultural value systems like *Utang na loob,* but I can push them aside. I know I am a new being in Christ. That's different. What controls me before cannot control me anymore because of my faith in Jesus Christ. That's why transformation is the solution to the problems in the Philippines. Education is a temporary measure. Transformation is an inward change we need.

I do not mean all Filipinos in the Philippines are victims or culprits of the downside of *Utang na loob.* Likewise, I do not mean all Filipino American Protestants in Texas are cultivating better cultural values. Rather, my interviewees show a seed of hope that people transformed by the power of the Holy Spirit through faith in Jesus can be the divine vehicle for transforming the downside of *Utang na loob* and unarticulated values.

Based on these Christian beliefs and convictions, as accentuated by Michel Foucault, everyday people should be able to generate alternative opposition voices to the dominant narratives that seem natural for the powerful to dominate and exploit the powerless. Countervailing discourses like the sacrificial love of Jesus on the cross, the story of self-giving, accountability, and mutuality was introduced in a theology of power of the chapter 2. Moreover, in the view of Hannah Arendt, to create alternative power structure, everyday people have to strive to "act and speak in concert" because she locates the source of power in "humans' capacity to act."[97] In the

97. Hinze, *Comprehending Power,* 127.

following chapter, I delve into how Filipino American Protestants in Texas will be able to be agents for this change.

CONCLUSION

In this chapter, I investigated two Filipino cultural values, that is, *Bahala na* and *Utang na loob*, which produce negative social imaginaries that generate and perpetuate a sense of powerlessness in the Philippines. My interviewees and some scholarly writings show that these two cultural values do function at some mythic level in relation to social imaginaries in the Philippines, and that there seems to be strong interrelationships between these social imaginaries and a sense of powerlessness. Furthermore, a sense of powerlessness results from a lack of agency inside people, and this agency is also strongly affected by social imaginaries in a society. In addition, these social imaginaries are birthed, nurtured, fortified, and practiced under the influence of the social system. For this reason, a sense of powerlessness is not only a matter of social structure, but also of social imaginary. Both of them should be explored as the main two causes for a sense of powerlessness.

My interviews discovered that *Bahala na*, on one hand, tends to be recognized as a fatalistic expression rather than agential. When people are confronted with challenging situations and hardship that are beyond their control, they utter this expression and consequently feed upon powerlessness of everyday people in the Philippines. This chapter explored the fatalistic religious background embedded in *Bahala na*, which had birthed, nurtured, and established *Bahala na*: animism, Hinduism, Islam, and Catholicism. On the other hand, some people argue that *Bahala na* can be also used in positive ways as a "shock absorber" in which people are willing to face their hardships and do their best to achieve their own goals. My interviews found that Filipino American Protestants in Texas do not utter *Bahala na* and they do not believe in destiny or fatalism. Rather, they view God as the One who helps those who help themselves. Two factors made this difference: their perspective in interpreting God's will and the awareness of agency in them.

Utang na loob is basically known in the Philippines as a good cultural value facilitating interpersonal solidarity development, and generosity in times of need among the relationships. However, it is usually created in beneficiary-benefactor relationships where the beneficiary feels subordinate to the benefactor. In this asymmetric relationship, *Utang na loob* functions as a social imaginary triggering and perpetuating a sense of powerlessness. Throughout my ethnographic research, I found out that Filipino American Protestants in Texas do not practice *Utang na loob* in the church, even though many other Filipinos in the Filipino community still do. It turned out that Filipino American Protestants in Texas have been able to transform the downside of *Utang na loob* because of their spiritual discipline and the power of the Holy Spirit.

In the following chapter, I focus on who Filipino American Protestants in Texas are. More specifically, in light of Diaspora Missiology and Agency Theory, I explore their missional agency to transform the Philippines.

5

Power and Diaspora Missional Agency

IN THE PREVIOUS TWO chapters, I presented two major causes that generate and perpetuate a sense of powerlessness for everyday people in the Philippines: structural evil and social imaginary. To verify these two factors, I referred to extensive literature and ethnographic research of Filipino American Protestants who were born and raised in the Philippines and then immigrated to Texas in the United States.

In this chapter, I focus on answering research question 3 as described in chapter 1, "How do US-based Protestant Filipinos in Texas perceive, negotiate, and exercise power? Do they believe the missional calling to transform the lives in the Philippines? If so, how do they respond to it?" Therefore, this chapter explores the missional agency of US-based Filipino Protestants in Texas as the agents who can bring about transformation in the Philippines. They do not live in the Philippines. Hence, they are not influenced by structural evil in the Philippines anymore. Even though they live in the United States, they are still aware of Filipino cultural values and even maintain some of them as well. Nevertheless, their cultural values have been negotiated, complemented, and modified by American cultural values.

Furthermore, I argue that their Protestant faith serves as the groundwork on which they understand, perceive, and exercise power, in ways different from that of Catholicism. Whereas Catholic Churches are dominant in the Philippines, Protestants can be an alternative group of people who can speak of the need for change and present specific pictures of change. I discovered that their Protestant faith inspires them to strongly believe in the transformation of the Philippines through the transforming power of God, and to desire to be the divine vessel for that transformation of their homeland. In this chapter, I explain this religious aspiration for transformation through the concept of missional agency and describe some potential changes triggered by them with respect to a sense of powerlessness in the Philippines.

Some people might wonder why this study focuses on the agency of Filipino American Protestants for the transformation of the Philippines; they might think that the agents for the change have to be sought and found in the homeland first and the actual transformation should come within the local people, not from outsiders. In the never-ending process of seeking the transformation of the Philippines, US-based Protestant Filipinos are one of many other ways to accomplish this goal. Moreover, this group of people has been barely spotlighted as a potential agent who can bring about the transformation of the Philippines. This is where this study intends to contribute to academia.

In this study, I suggest Filipino American Protestants as the transforming agents for the Philippines. As described in chapter 1, I found the existence of the *ladinos* who had been not only the cultural brokers but also cultural change agents between two different cultures (Spanish and Filipino, American and Filipino) during the country's respective colonial eras. Although they were originally not a ruling class, they rose to the upper class, and were even recognized later as the elite through their economic power, education, and socio-political networks. They found ways to navigate and make some changes to the power structures in the Philippines. Given the historical existence of the *ladinos* as culture brokers and culture changers, I argue that Filipino American Protestants represent the contemporary form of the *ladinos,* who brought about some alternative changes to power structures and social imaginaries in the Philippines. The potentiality of Filipino American Protestants as change agents centers on their bilingual capability with English and Tagalog (Filipino native language), high economic-educational status, professional careers, differentiated perception of power due to Protestantism, continuing connection with the mainland Philippines through some familial ties and organizational networks, and consequent dual identity between two different cultures (American and Filipino).

In what follows, I focus on Filipino American Protestants' missional agency in order to explain how they provide some helpful ways for confronting and negotiating a sense of powerlessness in the Philippines. For this study, I first describe the background of Filipino Americans such as the history of Filipino immigration to the USA, the phenomenon of Filipinos' global migration, and the characteristics of Filipino American *diasporas*. Then I present two theories, that is, Diaspora Missiology and Agency Theory whereby some substantial cases will be analyzed for how Filipino American Protestants exercise their missional agency.

THE HISTORY OF FILIPINO IMMIGRATION TO THE UNITED STATES

Investigating the missional agency of Filipino American Protestants leads to the need to know first who they are and how they came to the United States. For this, I explain the history of Filipino immigration to the United Sates with the help of the timeline by Daisy C.S. Catalan[1] and Luis F. Clement.[2] It can be summarized in four different phases: during Spanish rule, during American colonization, Post-Independence, and the Post-Immigration and Nationality Act of 1965.[3]

Four different Phases of Filipino Immigration to the United States

The first Filipino immigrants to the United States were known as the "Manila men and Luzones Indios" during Spanish rule.[4] These Filipinos were "shipbuilders, militiamen, navigators, sailors, slave laborers, and indentured servants who escaped from Spanish Galleons in the 16th century and settled in areas of California, Louisiana, and Mexico."[5]

The second phase of Filipino immigration occurred during the American colonization from 1898 to 1946. The colonization of the Philippines by the United States had a critical impact on Philippine migration. In 1898 toward the end of the Spanish-American War, Commodore George Dewey, American Navy Admiral, sailed to Manila. After a protracted period of conflict, "Spain ceded the Philippines to the United States at the Treaty of Paris" on December 10, 1898.[6] That marked the start of American colonization of

1. Catalan, "Diversity of the Filipinos."
2. Clement, *Running Head*, 20–22.
3. Remigio, "Demographic Survey," 27–29.
4. Cordova et al., *Filipinos: Forgotten Asian Americans.*
5. Cordova et al., *Filipinos: Forgotten Asian Americans.*
6. Catalan, "Diversity of the Filipinos."

the Philippines until their full independence was recognized with the inauguration of the Republic of the Philippines on July 4, 1946. In this phase, Filipino immigrants were called *Pensionados*, "the children of rich influential Filipinos who had good friendships with US officials, sent to study and work for services during World War I."[7] From 1906 to 1922, Filipinos were recruited to work as laborers in sugar plantations in Hawaii, as canners in Alaska, and as fruit and vegetable farmers in Washington and California.[8] These people were called *Manongs*.[9] In 1930, approximately 150 Filipinos became contract workers called *Sakadas*[10] in the sugar and pineapple plantations of Hawaii.[11] During Post-Depression and World War II from 1934 to 1945, the United States allowed 50 Filipinos every year to emigrate as permanent residents.[12] In 1945, the US Congress pass the War Brides Act of 1945, which allowed Filipinos who had enlisted in the United States Armed Forces to become legal residents of the United States.[13] In 1946, the Philippines became independent from the United States.

The third phase of Filipino immigration took place during Post-Independence from 1946 to 1965. The immigration quota was raised to 100 Filipinos per year immediately after independence. Due to the Immigration and Nationality Act, Filipinos were eligible for naturalization as US citizens after working three years in the United States Armed Forces. At the same time, the recruitment of plantation workers to Hawaii continued. From 1946 to 1965, more than 34,000 Filipinos migrated to the United States.[14]

The fourth phase of Filipino immigration from 1965 to 2000 began with the enactment of the Post-Immigration and Nationality Act of 1965. The United States officially began to accept immigrants of all nationalities on an equal basis; Filipino immigration to the United States increased in number. This new policy included "the admission of immediate relatives, the reunification of families, and the recruitment of needed skilled professional workers"[15] such as nurses, medical doctors, medical technologists,

7. Clement, *Running Head*, 20–22.

8. Catalan, "Diversity of the Filipinos."

9. Clement, *Running Head*, 20–22.

10. Clement, *Running Head*, 20–22.

11. Pedraza and Rumbaut, *Origins and Destinies*, 296.

12. Clement, *Running Head*, 20–22.

13. Cordova et al., *Filipinos.*

14. Catalan, "Diversity of the Filipinos."

15. Catalan, "Diversity of the Filipinos."

and teachers. During the 1980s, "more than half of the Filipino American population in the United States was foreign-born," mainly born in the Philippines.[16] During the 1990s, the Immigration and Naturalization Service (INS) reported one million Filipino admissions to the United States.[17]

The Fifth Phase of Filipino Immigration: 2001 to Present

I would like to add the fifth phase. In this phase, the pattern for Filipino immigration to the United States is similar to that of the fourth phase. The United States is still in need of skilled professional workers from overseas. Most of the new arrivals from the Philippines to the States are professionals such as nurses, doctors, medical technologists, teachers, and the like. In addition, many families and relatives of Filipino immigrants continue to move to the United States for the reunification of families.

According to U.S. Census Bureau 2011 American Community Survey, as of 2011, Filipinos represented the third largest immigrant[18] group (1,777,588) in the United States by country of origin behind Mexico (11,711,103), and India (1,780,322).[19] However, as of 2016, according to Migration Policy Institute (MPI), Filipino immigrants in the United States (1,942,000) ranked fourth in number, surpassed by Mexico (11,575,000), India (2,435,000), and China (2,130,000).[20] It seems that the US recently received more Chinese immigrants, who exceeded the number of Filipino immigrants. Although Filipinos' rank in number has declined from third to fourth, there has been a consistent increase in the number of Filipinos migrating to the United States for the past five years. This data demonstrates that the foreign-born Filipino immigrant population in the States is almost two million or over 4.4 percent of the entire foreign-born population of the nation. Moreover, it is noticeable that 69 percent of the adult Filipino

16. Catalan, "Diversity of the Filipinos."

17. Pedraza and Rumbaut, *Origins and Destinies*, 295.

18. According to Migration Policy Institute (MPI), the term "immigrants" (also known as the foreign-born) refers to people residing in the United States who were not U.S. citizens at birth. This population includes naturalized citizens, lawful permanent residents (LPRs), certain legal nonimmigrants (e.g., persons on student or work visas), those admitted under refugee or asylee status, and persons illegally residing in the United States.

19. Migration Policy Institute (MPI), "Largest Immigrant Groups." China (1,608,095), excluding Hong Kong and Taiwan, is ranked the 4th largest immigrant group right after the Philippines.

20. Migration Policy Institute (MPI).

American population is foreign-born, and an estimated 53 percent of the overall Filipino American community is foreign-born, mainly born in the Philippines.[21] What does this statistic imply? Why do Filipinos leave the Philippines and then move to the United States?

Why Filipinos move to the United States

"Filipinos-on-the-move" (migration of Filipinos) is one consequential phenomenon representing the pervasiveness of powerlessness deeply rooted in the Philippines. Every year over a million temporary workers leave the Philippines to work overseas in more than 190 countries. Perennially beset with high poverty levels, joblessness, and high underemployment rates, the Philippine government has supported migration as a means to alleviate their socio-economic hardships. In the words of Wan and Tira, Filipinos have been "pushed out by financial crisis and increasing political instability in the Philippines and pulled by promising jobs in other countries."[22] In 2016, according to the Philippine Statistics Authority, during the period from April to September, more than 2.2 million Filipinos left the Philippines to work abroad.[23] Thus, because of Overseas Filipinos Workers (OFWs), Filipinos have become one of the largest migrant populations in the world.[24] Filipinos are the world's second largest population of migrants living abroad (10,455,788), after Mexico.[25] Furthermore, the sheer labor power of Filipinos has been translated into money which is a universal form of value. Remittances of overseas Filipino workers accounted for 9.8 percent of the gross domestic product (GDP) in 2016.[26] According to World Bank Migration and Development Brief 27, the Philippines ranks third in 2016 among remittance receiving countries, just after India and China.[27]

The phenomenon of Filipinos-on-the-move is aligned with the global trend of migration. According to Jehu J. Hanciles, in the last half century, "South-North migration, involving swelling tides of guest workers, labor migrants, asylum seekers, political and economic refugees, as well as family

21. Cherry, *Faith, Family, and Filipino*, 15.
22. Wan and Tira, "Filipino Experience."
23. Survey on Overseas Filipinos 2016.
24. Agunias, *Linking Temporary Worker Schemes*; Migration Policy Institute.
25. World Bank, "Migration and Development Brief."
26. Inquirer, "Remittances of Overseas Filipino Workers."
27. World Bank Migration and Development Brief.

reunification, has been a dominant element in international migration."[28] Enoch Wan also states that people "move on voluntary basis" (for education, freedom, economic betterment, etc.) and are "being moved for involuntary reasons" (e.g. refugee, human trafficking, etc.).[29] In other words, "the combination of global integration and the ever-widening divide between the wealthy industrial North and the nations of the developing South has transformed the former into a magnet for migrant movement."[30] Of the numerous destinations for migrating Filipinos as of 2013 such as "Saudi Arabia (1,029,000), the United Arab Emirates (477,000), Canada (364,000), and Japan (226,000),"[31] the United States remains among the top draws.[32] According to the Pew Research Center, the Filipino population in the US in 2015 was estimated at 3,899,000, including both foreign-born and US-born Filipinos.[33] Filipinos are one of the active participants transforming American society "from a black-and-white affair to a multicolored reality."[34] As a matter of fact, their close historic ties to the U.S. military due to their American colonial experiences, and their prevalence in the medical and health-care professions in the US render Filipino immigrants distinguished among the other top five immigrant groups: Mexicans, Indians, Chinese, and Vietnamese.[35] What then are the major characteristics of Filipino American immigrants?

MAJOR CHARACTERISTICS OF FILIPINO AMERICAN IMMIGRANTS

This chapter narrows down some significant characteristics of Filipino Americans, which were previously mentioned as major factors related to power and powerlessness in the context of the Philippines.

---

28. Hanciles, "Migration and Mission," 118–29.
29. Wan, "Diaspora Missiology," 3–4.
30. Wan, "Diaspora Missiology," 3–4.
31. Migration Policy Institute (MPI), "Filipino Immigrants in the United States."
32. Cherry, *Faith, Family, and Filipino*, 16.
33. Pew Research Center, "Filipinos in the U.S. Fact Sheet."
34. Jenkins, *Next Christendom*, 126.
35. Migration Policy Institute (MPI), "Largest Immigrant Groups."

Economy, Employment, and Education

Philippine-born immigrants were less likely to live in poverty in 2015 than the native- or foreign-born overall. In 2015, according to the Pew Research Center, "a significantly smaller share of Filipino immigrants (6.3 percent) lived in households with an annual income below the official federal poverty line than the native-born (14.7 percent) and immigrants overall (17.8 percent)."[36] As of 2015, moreover, the median annual household income among Filipinos in the US is $80,000, based on $73,001 (for the US-born) and $83,000 (foreign-born).[37]

This data demonstrates the changing trend of Filipino's employment in the US. While "Filipino immigrants before 1965 were primarily low-wage laborers," now they are, mostly, "educated professionals" and tend to "be doing better socio-economically than many immigrant populations."[38] The educational attainment of foreign-born Filipinos in the US also supports this trend; 40 percent of them are college graduates, which is much higher than 19 percent of all Americans.[39] Moreover, according to the Migration Policy Institute (MPI), in 2013 "about 30 percent of Filipino immigrants (age 5 and over) reported limited English proficiency, compared with about 50 percent of the foreign born overall."[40] Their fluency in speaking English is one of the major reasons why so many Filipinos have been able to thrive in their professions, compared to other immigrant groups. Due to the American system of education established during the colonial era, Filipinos in the Philippines have been educated in English. In the labor market in the US, their fluency in English renders Filipino workers more favored than other immigrants who have a language barrier. Moreover, nearly one in every four employed immigrant Filipinas (female Filipinos) worked as a registered nurse in 2008, signifying that "women are an important part of the Filipino *diaspora* both culturally and economically."[41]

36. Pew Research Center, "Filipinos in the U.S. Fact Sheet."
37. Pew Research Center, "Filipinos in the U.S. Fact Sheet."
38. Cherry, *Faith, Family, and Filipino*, 15.
39. Pew Research Center, "Filipinos in the U.S. Fact Sheet."
40. Migration Policy Institute (MPI), "Filipino Immigrants in the United States."
41. Cherry, *Faith, Family, and Filipino*, 16.

Continual Connection with Homeland

Filipino American immigrants are basically transnational migrants. Ted C. Lewellen in *The Anthropology of Globalization* explains the concept of transnationalism:

> A transnational migrant is one who maintains active, ongoing interconnections in both the home and host countries and perhaps with communities in other countries as well . . . It is evident that transnationalism is thus a concept admitting of degrees; it may be intense—with constant phone calls, money transfers, back-and-forth travel, and participation in home politics and business.[42]

Filipino American immigrants continue to have contact with home in the Philippines, by sending numerous *balikbayan boxes* (care packages of assorted goods) and regular remittances, by watching Filipino news and TV shows, by participating in political elections through their familial networks,[43] and by engaging in civic movements via organizations. The transnationalism of Filipino American immigrants may involve the constant construction and reconstruction of a nation or *diaspora* community that transcends borders.[44] Although they move across national boundaries, Filipinos do not simply leave their homelands. Rather, they are able to "forge and maintain social relations at a distance across time and space,"[45] which link together their home and host societies. In other words, Filipino immigrants in the US often form what might be called *diasporic attachments* which refers to "dual affinity or double connection that mobile subjects have to localities, to their involvement in webs of cultural, political, and economics ties that encompass multiple national terrains."[46] They "belong to more than one world, speak more than one language (literally and metaphysically), inhabit more than one identity, and have more than one home."[47] They speak from the "in-between of different cultures, always unsettling the assumptions of one culture from the perspective of another,

---

42. Lewellen, *Anthropology of Globalization*, 151.

43. In my interviews, I found that some of them hold dual citizenship so that they are able to vote in political elections directly in the Philippines; Others hold only American citizenship so that they can impact political elections in the Philippines through their familial networks.

44. Lewellen, *Anthropology of Globalization*, 130.

45. Inda and Rosaldo, "Tracking Global Flows," 21.

46. Inda and Rosaldo, "Tracking Global Flows," 21.

47. Inda and Rosaldo, "Tracking Global Flows," 21.

and thus finding ways of being both *the same* and at the same time *different from* the others amongst whom they live."[48] In this sense, they have hybrid identities. Lorenzo, an interviewee, states, "We are hybrid. Yes, we are Americans and yet have another aspect of being Americans here in the US." I believe that their hybridity in identity has granted flexibility and resiliency to Filipinos immigrants between different cultures throughout the history of Spanish rule and American colonization, and even nowadays with their international migration in the globalized world.

Religious Affiliation

Above everything else, my attention was drawn to the great number of Filipino American Christians (Catholic 65 percent, Protestant 24 percent).[49] As the data shows, 24 percent of Filipino Americans are Protestants, a stark contrast with the fact that only 9.5 percent of Filipinos in the Philippines are Protestants (Catholic 80.6 percent).[50] The percentage of Filipino American Protestants (24 percent) fortifies the plausibility of transformation in the Philippines through Filipino American *diasporas*. Moreover, according to the Pew Research Center, Filipino Americans are the religiously least unaffiliated (8 percent) among U.S. Asian groups.[51] Stephen Cherry in *Faith, Family, and Filipino American Community Life* explores how the mutual interaction between their faith and family values strengthens their commitment towards civic engagement and how religion plays a crucial role in assisting immigrants in adjusting to their new environment since religion provides caring relationships and support to its adherents.[52] Religion also has the capacity to "foster community solidarity among migrants," which "could be best won by respecting diversity, a respect enacted in and through their small, culturally and linguistically homogenous fellowship groups."[53]

48. Hall, "New Cultures for Old," 175–213.

49. 89 percent of Filipino Americans are Christians: specifically, 65 percent are Catholics, and 24 percent are Protestants (evangelical 13 percent, mainline 9 percent, other Christian 3 percent); Refer to Pew Research Center, "Asian Americans: a mosaic of faith."

50. More than 90 percent of the population in the Philippines are Christians: about 80.6 percent belong to The Roman Catholic Church while about 9.5 percent belong to Protestant Christian denominations such as The United Methodist Church, The Baptist Church, The Philippine Independent Church, and United Church of Christ in the Philippines; Refer to Philippines in Figures: 2014.

51. Pew Research Center, "Asian Americans: A Mosaic of Faiths."

52. Cherry, *Faith, Family, and Filipino*.

53. Warner and Wittner, *Gatherings in Diaspora*, 369.

Thus, religion undoubtedly has a tremendous impact on the everyday life of Filipino immigrants in the US.

As described above, Filipino American immigrants are in general affluent, educated, professional in career, and religious. If so, what are the missiological implications of these characteristics? Why are they so significant for the transformation of lives in the Philippines? Diaspora Missiology has the answer for these questions.

DIASPORA MISSIOLOGY

Diaspora Missiology has emerged due to globalization, urbanization, the demographic shift of labor forces and immigration (from East to the West, South to the North), and Christian gravity (from global North to global South). As international migration has become a global phenomenon, *diasporas* were identified recently by Lausanne Movement leaders as a significant subfield in the study of missions. Sadiri Joy Tira (Filipino Canadian), and Enoch Wan (Chinese-Filipino American), key leaders of Diaspora Missiology in the Lausanne Movement, define Diaspora Missiology as "a missiological framework for understanding and participating in God's redemptive mission among people living outside their place of origin."[54] They understand that international migration (such as immigrants, transnational immigrants, *diasporas*, and even refugees) is under God's sovereign will for achieving the Great Mission in all nations. In this regard, Christian believers in *diaspora* can be motivated and mobilized for global missions. In light of Diaspora Missiology, Filipinos who have been dispersed to the United States are also under God's purpose to fulfill the Great Commission. We need to discern *diaspora* as a sign of the times and broaden the traditional paradigm to embrace *diaspora* missions as a creative strategic missionary force.

Key Concepts of Diaspora Missiology

According to Sadiri Joy Tira and Enoch Wan, "The integration of migration research and missiological study has resulted in practical '*diaspora* missiology'–a new strategy for missions. *Diaspora* mission is a providential and strategic way to minister to 'the nations' by the *diaspora* and through the *diaspora*."[55] In fact, *diaspora* missions have been taking place in many areas

---

54. Lausanne Movement, "Seoul Declaration."

55. Tira and Wan, "Filipino experience."

formerly untouched by traditional missions. Moreover, wherever Christian *diasporas* go and become a primary force giving witness to the Gospel and planting new churches, there has been amazingly consistent and dramatic growth of Christianity. The key concept of Diaspora Missiology is "ministering to *diaspora* groups (in evangelism and service) and ministering through/beyond them by motivating and mobilizing the church to fulfill the Great Commission."[56] More specifically, Wan classifies it into three types of *diaspora* missions: Missions *to the Diaspora*, Missions *through* the *Diaspora*, and Missions *by and beyond* the *Diaspora*.[57]

First, Mission *to the Diaspora* means "reaching the *diaspora* groups in forms of evangelism or pre-evangelistic social services, then disciple them to become worshipping communities and congregations."[58] This type implies that churches in host countries practice missions to newcomers in their neighborhoods without crossing borders geographically: "When God is moving the *diasporas* geographically and making them accessible, the Church should not miss any opportunity to reach them with the gospel."[59] Filipino Protestant churches associated with American denominations are the case for this–e.g. The Christian & Missionary Alliance Church, United Methodist Church, Baptist church, Lutheran Church and the like.

Second, Missions *through* the Diaspora means, "*diaspora* Christians reaching out to their kinsmen through networks of friendship and kinship in host countries, their homelands, and abroad."[60] Nowadays, Filipino American Churches of American-brand denominations undertake missions to their kinsmen in the US under the guidance of upper denominational authority, and at the same time have built their own networks and governing structures so that they autonomously do missions to kinsmen in the United States. In addition, Filipino American Churches' outreach to Filipinos in the Philippines fall under this type (Mission *through* Diaspora), especially when their homeland struggles with natural disasters and Filipino American churches send out rescue mission teams there. As missional agency is discussed in this chapter, mission through the Christian Filipino *diaspora* in the States to the homeland is the main focus in the later part of this chapter. However, this model needs to be

56. Wan and Tira, "Diaspora Missiology and Missions," 46–60.

57. Wan, *Diaspora Missiology*, 5.

58. Wan, *Diaspora Missiology*, 5.

59. Wan, *Diaspora Missiology*, 5.

60. Wan, *Diaspora Missiology*, 5.

more developed and implemented because Filipino American Protestants who belong to American Protestant denominations seem to have little power in the overall denominations. Some crucial examples presented in this chapter will usher in more plausible examples of this model to take place and consequently enhance their missional agency.

Third, mission *by and beyond* the *diaspora* implies "motivating and mobilizing *diaspora* Christians for cross-cultural missions to other ethnic groups in their host countries, homelands, and abroad."[61] The missions of Filipino American churches to the African American population and Hispanic people in the US are examples. Moreover, this model explains how some Filipino American churches have sent out Filipino Christians abroad as missionaries for both long and short terms to different locations in the world. By doing this, they posit themselves as a new type of social change agent in society, not just influencing the Philippines but also people of other races or ethnic groups.

In the following section, I will examine and analyze these three types of *diaspora* missions of Filipino American Protestants, based upon ethnographic interviews with Filipino American Protestants in Texas. For this ethnographic research, two churches in Dallas and Houston of Texas were randomly selected as the samples for investigating the missional agency of US-Based Filipino Protestants for the transformation of everyday people in the Philippines.

MISSIONAL AGENCY OF FILIPINO AMERICAN PROTESTANTS

With a focus on exploring the missional agency of Filipino American Protestants through the perspective of Filipino American Protestants in Texas, I first explain who they are, and then introduce Agency Theory. Then, I present my definition of missional agency through which three types of *diaspora* missions of the Filipino American *diaspora* will be examined and analyzed.

Filipino American diaspora in Texas

The first Filipino known by name in Texas was Francisco Flores, who came to Texas as a cabin boy on a merchant ship in 1822.[62] The Spanish-American

61. Wan, *Diaspora Missiology,* 5.
62. Texans One and All, "Filipino Texans."

War, at the end of the 19th century, was responsible for the first substantial entry of Filipinos to Texas. After acquiring the Philippines from Spain, the United States maintained a substantial number of US servicemen in the Philippines and these military officers hired a large number of Filipinos as servants. When those US servicemen returned to the United States, six Filipino employees followed them to San Antonio in Texas, which was recorded as "the first influx of Filipinos to Texas in 1910s."[63] Thereafter, in 1920, 30 male Filipino students came to Texas under a visiting program hosted by the United States to learn about democracy and the American way of life.[64] By 1930, the Filipino population continued to grow up to 288.[65] In 1945, the United States began to be an attractive destination for Filipino professionals such as "doctors, engineers, nurses, bankers, architects, accountants, pharmacists and so on."[66] In 1950, about 4,000 Filipinos were in Texas.[67] By 1960, 1,623 Filipinos lived in several cities like Beaumont, Port Arthur, Dallas, and Houston, which needed these new Filipino immigrants who were mostly professional female nurses and male doctors.[68] Others were the children of American military servicemen who married local Filipinas when they were stationed in the Philippines.[69] Unfortunately, these first Asian Texans faced discrimination until and even after the 1965 Immigration Act, which allowed extensive numbers of Filipinos to immigrate to the United States.[70]

Most Filipinos currently living in Texas are relatively recent arrivals. Since the 2000s, Texas has had one of the largest Filipino populations in the South.[71] According to Census 2010, "there are 137,713 Filipino Americans and Multiracial Filipino Americans in Texas."[72] In 2011, "five percent (86,400) of all Filipino immigrants in the United States lived in Texas."[73]

63. Texans One and All, "Filipino Texans."

64. Texans One and All, "Filipino Texans."

65. Fifteenth Census of The United States 1930, "Table 20," 59.

66. Gallery of Texas Cultures, "Filipino Texans."

67. Brady, *Asian Texans*, 73.

68. Texans One and All, "Filipino Texans."

69. Gallery of Texas Cultures, "Filipino Texans."

70. Gallery of Texas Cultures, "Filipino Texans."

71. Brady, *Asian Texans*, 73.

72. United States Census Bureau, "Profile of General Population and Housing Characteristics: 2010."

73. Stoney and Batalova, "Filipino Immigrants."

As more Filipino Americans came to Texas, the center of their population shifted to Houston as Texas Medical Center in Houston grew and Houston became home to about 2,000 Filipino nurses. Houston (Houston-Sugar Land-Baytown) has the largest population of Filipino Americans (47,926)[74] in the South and Arlington (Dallas-Fort Worth-Arlington) ranks second in number (33,206).[75] According to Marilyn D. Brady, due to Texas being part of the Bible Belt, it has been a popular destination for emigrating Filipino Protestants,[76] with their theological conservative tendency.

Considering the history of Filipino immigration to the United States, unlike the West Coast, Texas lacks the historical foundations of pre-1965 Filipino immigration. Moreover, Filipinos in Dallas (Arlington) and Houston are comparatively new arrivals, and their communities are less established. For this reason, they have much stronger connections with the Philippines. Many of them are well educated, professional in employment, highly paid, and highly fluent in English and Tagalog (national indigenous language). Therefore, those living in these two cities in Texas serve as excellent cases for studying the sense of powerlessness, structural evil, and social imaginary in the Philippines. Furthermore, as I argue that the Filipino American diaspora can be a contemporary form of the *ladinos*, Filipino immigrants in Texas seem to be a more plausible example for this case.

In my ethnographic research on the Filipino American Protestants, classifying 31 participants by occupation, there are 5 registered nurses, 1 nurse practitioner, 1 pharmacist, 2 medical technologists, 4 medical and health care workers, 5 engineers, 3 accountants, 1 educator, 4 office managers, 2 clergyperson, 2 church workers, and 1 deputy sheriff. It turned out that 13 out of 31 participants or more than 40 percent (41.9 percent) work in the medical field. Moreover, in classifying them by gender and occupation, 5 out of 16 female interviewees or 31.2 percent of them are registered nurses, and in total 9 of 16 or 56.25 percent of female participants work in the medical field. This information verifies the literature described above. Thus, Filipino American immigrants in Texas seem highly empowered. From the perspective of agency theory, they exercise agency with the high level of personal efficacy.

---

74. Pew Research Center, "Filipinos in the U.S. Fact Sheet."

75. Pew Research Center, "Filipinos in the U.S. Fact Sheet."

76. Brady, *Asian Texans*, 72.

Agency Theory

In social science, agency is usually defined as "the capacity of individuals to act independently and to make their own free choices."[77] Agency is influenced by structural factors such as social class, religion, gender, ability, and customs, even though it is uncertain to what extent social systems constrain people's actions. In this sense, agency theory "concerns the nature of individual freedom in the face of social constraints, the role of socialization in the forming of 'persons,' and the place of particular ways of doing things in the reproduction of cultures."[78] In short, "agency theory is about the relationships among human beings, and between individuals and their surroundings."[79]

The literature on agency across social sciences is vast and expanding nowadays. Anthony Giddens and Pierre Bourdieu are the leading figures among contemporary theorists of agency who have attempted to "unite 'the individual' (agency) and 'the social' (structure) within a single analytical framework."[80] However, Giddens has been accused of making his actors "too self-oriented, with too much self-reflexivity and potential for self-mastery."[81] Therefore, other theorists of agency questioned, "whether the term agency refers to an essential property of individuals, or whether it lies somehow in the relationships between individuals with a possibility that might also afford us a notion of collective agency."[82] In this way, we have the potential to provide "not only a social account of selfhood, but also an account of how groups of people can come to develop their own agentic capabilities."[83] This concept rationalizes the need that the agency of US based Filipino Protestants can be conceived in light of a notion of collective agency. According to Martin Hewson, there are three types of agency: individual, proxy, and collective.[84] Whereas individual agency generates when an individual acts on his/her own behalf, proxy agency is exercised when

---

77. Baker, *Cultural Studies*, 448.
78. Baker, *Cultural Studies*, 448.
79. Baker, *Cultural Studies*, 448.
80. Baker, *Cultural Studies*, 448.
81. Baker, *Cultural Studies*, 3.
82. Baker, *Cultural Studies*, 3.
83. Baker, *Cultural Studies*, 4.
84. Hewson, "Agency," 13–17.

a person acts on behalf of someone else.[85] Collective agency occurs when people act together, such as a social movement.[86]

The distinction between individual and collective agency and the emphasis on both shed a new light on how to approach the discussion on the missional agency of Filipino American Protestants. We need to focus not only on their individual agency but also on the collective agency of Filipino American Protestants as a *diaspora* group. Throughout my ethnographic research, I found that Filipino American immigrants exercise a high level of individual agency in terms of education, occupation, and economic status. However, I realized that proxy agency and collective agency of Filipino American immigrants have not been investigated very well as agents for the transformation of the Philippines. As a matter of fact, as many Filipino scholars lament, Filipino Americans are all but an "invisible and silent minority" and the "forgotten Asian Americans," whose increasing presence has been neglected in intercultural studies as well.[87] Although Filipino American immigrants have been introduced as one of many other people-on-the-move, they have been rarely spotlighted as the crucial key player in Diaspora Missiology. Here is where this chapter can contribute to the literature on Diaspora Missiology with special reference to Filipino American immigrants.

Agency and Power

The term agency usually has something to do with power. Hewson identifies three properties of human beings that give rise to agency: intentionality, power, and rationality.[88] Human beings act with intention, and their different abilities produce different levels of agency. As a result, human beings are guided by their intellect for predicting the results of their actions. For better understanding of agency and power, it is common and useful to distinguish between "power-over"–i.e. the ability to affect what someone else does or "the capacity to act *against* or *in spite of* others"[89]– and "power to"–i.e. "the capability to decide actions and carry them out."[90] Giddens perceives that every human agent holds some modicum of

85. Hewson, "Agency," 13–17.

86. Hewson, "Agency," 13–17.

87. Cordova, *Filipinos: Forgotten Americans*; Espiritu, *Home Bound*.

88. Hewson, "Agency," 13–17.

89. Hinze, *Comprehending Power*, 5.

90. Green, *From Poverty to Power*, 25.

power-to or power-over to a degree to make "a knowledgeable difference in a relationship."[91] I think agency theory falls somewhere in between power-over and power-to with a focus more on the latter. According to Gardner, two critical issues that should be considered in the discourse of agency and power are choice and intentionality.[92]

AGENCY AND DUAL IDENTITY

As mentioned earlier, Filipino immigrants in the States possess a hybrid identity. They belong to more than one world, speak more than one language, and inhabit more than one identity. They constantly construct and re-construct their homeland and the Filipino *diaspora* community in the United States. In this process, they exercise their proxy agency, which means that they act on behalf of Filipino families in the Philippines, especially for financial support. They also exercise their collective agency by establishing some organizations to help and transform the lives in the Philippines.

There is, for example, a Filipino American organization called FAITH (Filipino-American Initiative to Transform our Homeland), which was introduced to me by one of the participants in my ethnographic interview. FAITH, which was inaugurated on September 19, 2015, and led by Eustaquio Abay, MD, a neurosurgeon in Kansas, "aims to establish and develop a working partnership with the Philippine government for the necessary transformation of the country for the ultimate benefits of the people, especially the marginalized and those suffering in the gutter of poverty."[93] They have five specific goals:

> 1) Make medical/surgical missions more efficient and sustainable.
> 2) Establish and develop a working partnership with Philippine government and its agencies with clearly defined projects. 3) Connect and collaborate with as many Filipino American groups and organizations (US, Canada and elsewhere) as possible. 4) Encourage our youth and young adults to visit the Philippines, discover their roots, and learn about their culture and heritage first hand. Be inspired. 5) Encourage Filipino American adults and retirees to revisit and rekindle their love of country.[94]

91. Hinze, *Comprehending Power,* 157.

92. Gardner, *Agency Uncovered,* 5.

93. LA Weekend Asian Journal.

94. LA Weekend Asian Journal.

FAITH is one great example of how their dual identity fortifies their proxy agency and collective agency.

One question arises: "Why do they maintain diasporic attachments and aspire for constant connection with their homeland and its transformation?" This question arose out of the tendency that most of the participants in my ethnographic research, even though many of them gained American citizenship, identify themselves as Filipinos rather than Americans. Luz, an interviewee, describes the reason why she prefers being Filipino to being American:

> By blood and by heart I am Filipino, but right now by status I'm American . . . I think my culture is better. I mean the way we were raised by our family, by our parents, because here we can see how American kids treat their parents, how they want to be out of their parents' home when they turn 18 because they want to do whatever they want to do. There is no respect. But we treat older people with respect even if we don't like them.

She seems to be proud of being Filipino in terms of culture and intentionally chooses to be more Filipino than American. According to Thomas H. Eriksen in *Ethnicity and Nationalism,* this pride in being Filipino takes place because of ethnic identity. He states, "Ethnic identities, which embody a perceived continuity with the past, may in this way function in a psychologically reassuring way for the individual in times of upheaval."[95] In the case of Filipino American immigrants, upheaval times most likely are the times of marginalization, racial discrimination, and social isolation in the host country. In order to be assured in times of upheaval, they have to find a continuous connection with the past. The solution is through ethnic identities. To clarify this concept, Eriksen mentioned the phrase *ethnic belongingness.* Eriksen explains that maintaining one's ethnic identity leads people to recognize their ethnic belongingness that can be an important source of "self-respect" and "personal authenticity" in the globalized world.[96] Therefore, in sum, Filipino American *diasporas* exercise proxy agency and collective agency through their Filipino ethnic identity whereby they can find self-respect and personal authenticity even though they are American citizens. I argue that their continuous self-identifying process affords them the inspiration to discover their agency for change and see themselves as agents for transformation of the homeland.

95. Eriksen, *Ethnicity and Nationalism,* 68.
96. Eriksen, *Ethnicity and Nationalism,* 68.

Then, my last question is, "What can Filipino American Protestants and their Church do to bring about the transformation of the Philippines?" I suggest missional agency as the answer to this question.

Missional Agency

The agency of Filipino American Protestants can be fostered and enhanced not only through dual identity and strong connection with the homeland, but also by their Protestant faith that invites them to accomplish the Great Commission. I named this *Missional Agency*, defined as the capability of Christians as individuals and the Church as a whole to intentionally make their own free choice of participating in God's mission regardless of the external constraints. Moreover, as mentioned, the hybrid identity of Filipino American Protestants, between two different countries and transnationalism, renders their missional agency more validated and maximized. When I asked my participants in the interviews about their calling to transform the Philippines, almost everyone confirmed it with no hesitation. Patria, an interviewee, answers:

> In our women's ministry, we have been supporting a newly planted church in the Philippines. Every time we have a meeting, I encourage the women to make sure we remember the sister church in the Philippines, and we are helping them to grow and get their lives better by our hearts, our prayers and our financial help. So now we already have that mindset and can be part of mission even though we are not physically there. They will also come to the Lord. We are already missiologists a little bit!

Her words demonstrate the missional agency of Filipino American Protestants who are willing to participate in God's mission to transform lives in the Philippines, despite the external constraints, that is, physical absence from the homeland. Lyndon, an interviewee, also states: "I want to highlight the potential to reach out to our brothers and sisters in the Philippines. The main thing is the desire to do it. We have to be aware of it. More awareness is the factor . . . I know that God wants me to give back to the Philippines. When we plan our retirement, it will be a heavily dedicated ministry." Lyndon's words such as "desire," and "awareness" connote the meaning of missional agency. Reggie, an interviewee, also maintains, "God looks at each one of us as God's representatives, God's agent in this world. We have to develop the attitude in the church like "How can we help?" . . . Filipino American Churches need to be intentional to support their mission works for the poor churches in the Philippines. Do it intentionally." The word "intentionally" or "intentional" echoes the core meaning of missional agency.

In what follows, I probe the missional agency of Filipino American Protestants through the framework of Diaspora Missiology. However, I limit its scope to only two types: Mission *through* Diaspora, and Mission *by/beyond* Diaspora because this study focuses mainly on Filipino American Protestants' missional agency for transformation of the Philippines, which conforms to these two models.

MISSION *THROUGH* DIASPORA

This type indicates that Filipino American Protestants reach out to their fellow Filipinos through the networks of friendship and kinship in host countries, their homelands, and abroad.

Empowering Filipinos through education. Filipinos tend to place great weight upon the importance of education in terms of empowerment and promotion in status. For Filipinos, as one qualitative study testifies, education is traditionally regarded as a symbolic and practical way of jumping into a higher class.[97] In the same alignment, Filipino American Protestants also believe that education is one of the powerful ways for Filipinos to gain more power and enhance their awareness.

In my interviews, 31 participants were asked to answer this question: "What gives people power?" The most influential power source for Filipino American Protestants turned out to be money (18 out of 31 participants chose money), political position (6), education (4), family background (2), voice-out (1). However, when my participants were given the chance to choose multiple factors, 15 participants, or 48.3 percent of all the participants, mentioned education as one of the most powerful factors that give people power. Why is money more important than anything else in terms of power? As I already explained in chapter 3, everyday people in the Philippines are limited to connecting with the sponsors because powerful people tend to stick together by themselves. Therefore, it is only through money that they can purchase the status of a patron and overcome a sense of powerlessness, whereas in the past the status was inherited. Moreover, education is also mentioned as one of the most influential power sources. However, being educated still requires money. Ironically, education gives

97. Tuason, "Those Who Were Born Poor," 52.

power to people, but without money, they cannot be educated. Therefore, the donation of scholarships for educating the Filipino young generation is of a great help for Filipinos to be empowered, who might otherwise have felt a sense of powerlessness.

Lorenzo, an interviewee, states that his church started a scholarship foundation to support Filipino students, churches, pastors, and a Bible school in the Philippines: "Actually one of our leaders here established a scholarship foundation. She has raised money here in Texas for the indigent children in the Philippines to help start their schooling and get to have some money to buy school supplies." Luz, an interviewee, states: "Education is the important factor in terms of power in the Philippines . . . . Through education they can be knowledgeable and know what to say and what to do. If you have knowledge, you have power. Without knowledge, there is no power." Luz's words exactly represent the concept of Anthony Giddens, that is, the "knowledgeability" which points to the importance of understanding how to gain power in social patterns. Carmelita, an interviewee, shared her calling from God to put up an orphanage for educating and caring for the street children in Bulacan, her hometown in the Philippines, because she believes that children are the future of the Philippines: "That is why we have to start with the children always . . . That's going to be my mission. God has been calling me to do it. Money wise, $20,000 will be good enough to start this mission. I cannot transform all the children, but I can start with ten at least." In this sense, as Filipino American Protestants believe that money and education are two of the most powerful factors that give people power, providing Filipino students with scholarships (money) for better education is one of the best ways to empower Filipinos in the Philippines for transforming the asymmetric structure of power in the Philippines.

Education can transform the Philippines possibly by increasing the awareness of people about the structural evil and social imaginary that cause and perpetuate a sense of powerlessness. Lyndon gives his example of how education can help increase people's awareness of structural issues and be active in contributing to the change:

> Most people feel powerless in the Philippines. Technically there is nothing through which they can express their power except through voting in political elections. But, they always vote for the popular candidate. It's not an educated vote. Why is it so? It is because they are not educated enough . . . . I came from a school, University of the Philippines. There I was trained how to fight against the dictator back in the '80s. I know how to plan, how to

get on with other people like me, and how to change. I know how
it feels to be part of that voice.

In the same vein, education in the context of the Philippines is meant to
restore human dignity to those who feel powerless because education gives
people more power. Education also grants them gifts that contribute to
the well-being of themselves and their community because people can be
equipped to be professional in career through education.

One question arises here: "how does education get this significant
role in giving people power in the Philippines?" Robert D. Woodberry
gives a hint at the answer. Woodberry argues that Protestantism, particularly "Conversionary Protestants (CP),"[98] were "a crucial catalyst that
initiated the development and spread of religious liberty, mass education,
mass printing, newspapers, voluntary organizations and most major colonial reforms."[99] According to Woodberry, since Conversionary Protestants (CP) advocated mass literacy so that everyone could read the Bible,
"their attempt to convert people through education threatened other elites
and spurred these elites to also invest in mass education."[100] I believe that
Woodberry's argument is the case in the Philippines as well because as
Susan K. Harris states, "Many of the early American teachers to reach the
Philippines were Protestant missionaries."[101] In this regard, I would like
to underscore the influence of Protestant Christianity upon this type of
education in the Philippines. During the American colonial period, more
than one thousand American civil educators, known as the *Thomasites*, arrived in the Philippines from 1901 to 1902 to set up a free primary public
education system, to train Filipino teachers, to render English the major
medium of instruction.[102] In the Philippines, compared to the educational
system of the former Spanish rule which benefited only the elites' children, "American democratic emphasis on public mass education instilled
into Filipinos a desire for upward social mobility."[103] Since the early years

---

98. Woodberry, "Missionary Roots of Liberal Democracy," 244–74; According to
Woodberry, the term "Conversionary Protestants (CP)" refers to those who actively wit-
nessed faith, emphasized lay persons reading the Bible in their own language, and believe
that grace/faith/choice saves people rather than group memberships or sacraments.

99. Woodberry, "Missionary Roots of Liberal Democracy," 245–46.

100. Woodberry, "Missionary Roots of Liberal Democracy," 251.

101. Harris, *God's Arbiters*, 219.

102. Francia, *History of the Philippines*, 165; Karnow, *In Our Image*.

103. "Philippines—History and Background."

of the American colonial period, for the Filipinos, earning a diploma ensured a good job and acceptance in society with a chance for a better future. Thus, in the Philippines, Protestantism influenced social mobility through education and consequently education became recognized as one of the most powerful factors to give people power. Therefore, I argue that Filipino American Protestants empowering Filipinos through education is very Protestant in its nature and is one of the most effective ways to help everyday people to be empowered. Although someone might argue that Catholics nowadays are also very involved in education, in this study I focus only on the particulars of Protestant education.

Seeking spiritual transformation through raising spiritual leaders. Several participants mentioned that education is not an absolute solution to the situation in the Philippines, but a conversion or transformation. Reggie, an interviewee, states: "Education is not the solution. The solution is a conversion or transformation. Unless the hearts of people, especially of political leaders, are converted or transformed from within, the present ways of life in the Philippines will be the same as the way they used to." Lyndon, an interviewee, also maintains that raising "a man of integrity and character" is the best way to transform the Philippines:

> What I'm looking for is a person with integrity and character. Then change can happen . . . I think it's possible if we mobilize the evangelical churches here [US] to help our evangelical brethren in the Philippine to get educated and enhance their awareness of speaking up for the political issues. I think we can regain the voice if we put a born-again Christian in leadership. Can you imagine the kind of change that he can do for the country?

Most Filipino Americans like Lyndon do not have any direct influence over anything in the Philippines. Instead, they are aware of the strong need for spiritual transformation of Filipinos, especially political leaders in the Philippines.

One of the ways for fulfilling this purpose is to specifically support seminaries, pastors, and church leaders in the Philippines so that spiritual leaders will not only be educated as the ones with integrity and character, but also be able to raise these kinds of people for the transformation of the Philippines. Lorenzo, an interviewee, states, "We are also a part of raising money to rebuild some of the Bible school buildings in Zamboanga, which are 78 years old . . . The Bible school is a training ground for future pastors and missionaries. So that's important." According to Lorenzo, when he and his church heard about the news that the students at a seminary in the Philippines could not afford to buy a copy of the Bible, which crucially affected the efficiency of their ministry, his church through the scholarship foundation sent them numerous Bibles. Lorenzo states, "What we can do here is to support the evangelization of the people in the Philippines. If they become Christians, then their hearts will be changed. If people's hearts are changed, then they become change agents in their society. They will become different people. Instead of participating in the corruption, they would say, "No, we should not do that."" Some of his words seem to reflect the evangelical American way of undertaking social change: "Win someone's heart for the Lord, and you will win the entire nation!" However, it has its own shortcomings. I believe that changing people's hearts (evangelism) should be accompanied by changing social structures (social transformation) at the same time. For the systemic transformation of the Philippines, they need to develop the types of power-with, that is, the power to work through organizational networks by which they will pursue some tangible changes in social systems at the government level.

Nevertheless, for Filipino American Protestants, educating and raising spiritual leaders in partnership with local churches in the Philippines can be an incipient stage to beginning the discourse on how to change people's hearts and then empowering them to be the change agents for the Philippines. This point highlights an important shift in the focus of transformational development because the point of greatest transformational leverage is changed people: "It is a transformed person who transforms his or her environment."[104] People, neither money nor education, transform their world. In this sense, it is noticeable that Filipino American Protestants in my research pointed out spiritual transformation as one of the major keys for the transformation of the Philippines, and focused on exercising their missional agency for this purpose.

Sending a rescue mission team to the Philippines. One of the ways for Filipino American Protestants to exercise their missional agency is to actively help victims of natural disasters in the Philippines. When Typhoon Haiyan smashed into the city of Tacloban in the central Philippines in 2013, One Filipino American church I interviewed sent out their mission team to Tacloban to help restore the devastated city. Jerico explains, "We went there

104. Musopole, "African World View," 2.

not only to conduct medical and dental services and distribute handouts like foods and clothes, but also to create a livelihood project there to sustain local people." For the livelihood projects, this church provided a certain amount of money to a local church in Tacloban. The local church used that money to buy four tricycles, which is a form of Filipino public transportation, and then gave them to four different families so that they could generate income. Jerico explains, "If one family could earn 400 pesos, 100 pesos would go to the church and the family would get 300 pesos. The family has been financially provided and the church also has something from this project. If this church can take care of it, they can buy another tricycle and then give it to another family." This Filipino American Church had helped Filipinos through a format of sustainable development. Jerico testified that this livelihood project through a local church in Tacloban had greatly influenced the lives of the church members, and also inspired the church to reach out to their local community. As a matter of fact, some of the beneficiaries in this project became members of the church. This is one great example, implemented by Filipino American Protestants partnering with a local church in the Philippines, of viewing the local churches and particularly the church of the poor as "the primary agents of holistic mission" and ascertaining that "there can be no sustainable Christian development that is distinctly Christian without sustainable Christian communities."[105]

To fundraise for the missions in Tacloban, the Filipino American church in Houston intentionally chose to be the agent for collecting money and was able to raise $17,000 from different churches through networks with their local communities and other Filipino American churches. Noticeably, Vietnamese neighbors in that local community were inspired by the missional agency of this Filipino church and donated $400,000 (which does not include the $17,000 mentioned above) for helping the victims in Tacloban. This is one great example of the Filipino *diaspora* in the States demonstrating how they exercise their missional agency not only as individuals but also as a collective community. Filipino American Protestants have the potential to provide not only a social account of selfhood, but also an account of how they as a group of people can come to develop their own agentic capabilities even in partnership with other immigrant communities.[106] This case successfully ascertains that a collective agency

105. Chester et al., *Justice, Mercy, and Humility*, 8.
106. Gardner, *Agency Uncovered*, 4.

is possible, which was questioned and theorized by Andrew Garner[107] and Martin Hewson (three types of agency).[108]

Networking with other organizations to impact the Philippines. As mentioned above, Filipino American Protestants eagerly anticipate the leaders of integrity and character sitting on political positions. There are some Filipino American organizations in which they can voice out on certain political issues, particularly for presidential elections in the Philippines. A participant in my research joined one of these organizations, called *US Pinoy 4 Good Governance*, which was originally organized as a fundraising organization for the candidacy of Benigno Aquino III for president in the 2010 national elections and later on became a watchdog for Aqunio's presidency. One of my interviewees was also invited to attend the inauguration of President Aquino and the forums for three days in Manila, the Philippines in 2010. US Pinoy 4 Good Governance pursues at least two expectations: "the first is for participants to come to a consensus on how to increase positive political influence in the Philippines even as they live and work abroad; the second is to connect and network among participants so we can unite and work together for good governance . . . . We were inspired by the essential truth in P-Noy's campaign slogan of *"kung walang corrupt, walang mahirap,"* or "If there is no corruption, there is no poverty."[109] This demonstrates one of the examples of how Filipino American Protestants can exercise their missional agency in the political arena of the Philippines through organizational networks, which Duncan Green calls *"power-with."*[110] This is also reminiscent of the message of James D. Hunter: "Christians should not ignore the opportunity that the institutions of society have far more potential to influence culture than do individuals alone."[111] From the perspective of Hannah Arendt, when they "act and speak in concert" through "a web of relationships" to push the government "to serve and protect public space," their missional agency in a public sphere generates and fosters political action and power-to.[112] In Arendt's eyes, Filipino American Protestants are demonstrating a much more constructive view of the relationship between

107. Gardner, *Agency Uncovered*, 3.
108. Hewson, "Agency," 13–17.
109. Office of the President of the Philippines, "Commission on Filipinos Overseas."
110. Green, *From Poverty to Power*, 25.
111. Hunter, *To Change the World*, 32.
112. Hinze, *Comprehending Power*, 139.

agency and power in the public sphere. Thus, the missional agency of Filipino American Protestants is exercised and enhanced when they unite into networks, coalitions, and even larger associations.

As we observed how Filipino American Protestants have been involved in God's mission for the transformation of the Philippines, the same question arises: "Why do they want to do this?" Not only their transnationalism and dual identity, but also their Protestant theology undergirding God's calling to the Great Commission fosters and reinforces their intentional desire to be divine instruments for the transformation of the Philippines.

Regardless of some successful cases with great potentiality, their power to execute missions is still incipient. Reggie, an interviewee, pinpoints this: "Filipino American Christians in the US know a lot of knowledge, but they are very slow in applying the knowledge. So, application is lacking. They can tell what needs to be done. But when we say, "Let's do it," they are very slow in doing that." Nonetheless, he suggests that a good place to begin is through the networks of local churches and other community organizations in America and the Philippines:

> This change begins with local churches. You educate them, and teach them with the community organizations. You already have some fellow believers in the local churches, and then continue to have networking and connection with other Christians. You can work better through organizational networks with other churches and organizations. We cannot do it alone.

He reflects the words of James D. Hunter throughout his own experiences: "the institutions of society have far more potential to influence culture than do individuals alone."[113] Thus, there are some great potential for Filipino Americans to trigger tangible changes in the Philippines through organizational networks. However, it seems to be just a beginning stage and needs to be more elaborated, organized, and developed for consistent visible outcomes in the future.

MISSION BY/BEYOND DIASPORA

This type indicates that Filipino American Protestants motivate and mobilize their kinsmen for cross-cultural missions to other ethnic groups in their host countries, homelands, and abroad.

---

113. Hunter, *To Change the World*, 32.

Church as a Community Center. Reggie, an interviewee, maintains the significance of a mission-minded attitude for the church: "We as the church should be willing to say, 'Okay, use us to help these people! We are willing to help!' God created us and saved us for what? It is to serve the common good, to serve people. This is what the church is all about. This is the mission of the church to lift up the orphans, the needy, and the poor. That is why we put up a community center first and then built our Sanctuary." This church in Houston has provided a senior program from Monday to Friday in partnership with the YWCA. What drew my attention was that this senior program was not just for Filipino American seniors but every individual senior in the local community. As I observed, there were Vietnamese, Chinese, Filipino, and American seniors in the senior program of this church. I believe that the hybrid identities of Filipino Americans enabled them to reach out and embrace other ethnic groups and facilitated this multicultural ministry to take place in their local communities. As George Yancey ascertains that whites attending multiracial churches exhibit less social distance toward other ethnic groups and have a lower tendency to hold stereotypes,[114] this multiracial ministry by a Filipino American congregation in Houston may have a significant impact on racial attitudes and actions, and therefore racial relations in the United States. In this sense, the periphery (Filipino Americans and other ethnic groups) has set itself up within the very heart of the West (Houston) and therefore the core has been "peripheralized."[115] Thus, Filipino American Protestants faithfully exercise their missional agency to fulfill God's mission to other ethnic groups in their local communities.

Church reaching out to other ethnic groups locally and globally. Lorenzo, an interviewee, states that his church sent out a missionary to a small island in the Pacific. Lorenzo states: "Our Mission's Chairperson eventually left everything that she was doing in Dallas and decided to be a missionary to Rota, a small island in the Pacific near Saipan. She started to be a teacher and eventually became the principal of the school. It was a mission school targeting the poor and marginalized on this little island." This church has been involved in this global mission by prayer and fundraising. On top of that, according to Lorenzo, this church contributed not less than $10,000 every year to the Global Mission Funds in their denomination to help

114. Yancey, "Examination of the Effects," 279–304.
115. Inda and Rosaldo, "Tracking Global Flows," 6–21.

deploy their missionaries worldwide. When it comes to local missions, this church has participated in Habitat for Humanity where a group from this church goes to a predominantly black neighborhood in Fort Worth and helps them rebuild their homes.

Church embracing a Hispanic congregation as their church family. I believe that the utmost level of missional agency can be measured by how engaged they are in cross-cultural ministries. Some people might argue that this case does not pertain to the goal of this study, that is, to explore how US-based Filipino Protestants impact the Philippines. Nevertheless, I believe that this case is significant in a way to understand the extent to which Filipino American Protestants can exercise missional agency, and to indirectly describe their implicit potential missional agency for the transformation of the Philippines.

Fortunately, from my interviewee I heard an amazing story for this case and was able to contact the pastor of a Filipino American Church in California. The pastor articulates:

> One Hispanic pastor wanted to meet with me and requested to rent from our church. That Hispanic congregation wanted to use our building in the afternoon for their Sunday worship service . . . After one year with this setting, the pastor had to resign and then many of the church members left. So, this Hispanic congregation started to talk to me and wanted to come under my leadership. In three months, I had to prepare the possible merger between our Filipino American Church and that Hispanic congregation.

The initial reaction of the Filipino Church Board, according to the pastor, was negative. As Emerson and Kim point out, "For members of an ethnic church who seek to preserve cultural traditions and pass them onto their children, a multiracial congregation is not necessarily desirable."[116] In fact, many ethnic church members were initially attracted to their churches because of the opportunity for ethnic fellowship. For this reason, the pastor began to work with them on some theological understanding of their mission as a church of God. The pastor of that church states: "Our mission is to love God, love others and serve the world. For the succeeding months, my preaching had revolved around this theme: how we are equal at the foot of the cross, being hospitable to the strangers/foreigners as many of them are undocumented, and why our love for others should not be just

116. Emerson and Kim, "Multicultural Congregation," 217–27.

a lip service but action required which can make us inconvenienced." After three months, the Filipino church was ready to receive the Hispanic congregation as their church family. Their church attendance doubled and continued to grow, especially on the Hispanic side. Their worship service is presided in English, and translation service is provided through headsets. The pastor explains the beauty of diversity in his church: "During our worship service, we sing two songs in Spanish, two songs in English. Our worship team is made up with different nationalities. Congo player is Peruvian, keyboardist is Russian, bassist is Filipino American, guitarist is Mexican, drummer is El Salvadorian, and backup singers are Filipino and Nicaraguan." The pastor said, "The initial months had been thorny but with open dialogue and the desire to find a common ground under the Lordship of Jesus Christ over our church, we were able to solve conflicts." The pastor with his church demonstrates the biblical exercise of power. Jesus was the center in their understanding and exercising of power so that they were able to serve and embrace other ethnic groups.

In the words of Jung Young Lee in *Marginality*, this case demonstrates that Filipino American Protestants as transnational migrants overcome the marginality of other transnational migrants through their marginality. Lee states, "Marginality is overcome through marginality. When all of us are marginal, love becomes the norm of our lives . . . We then become servants to one another in love."[117] This case also illustrates how "the Ephesian moment" of Andrew Walls looks like, which means, "the social coming together of people of two cultures to experience Christ" whereby "believers from the different communities are different bricks being used for the construction of a single building–a temple where the One God would live (Ephesians 2:19–22)."[118] In other words, each one of the various different ethnic identities in this church is used as one brick for constructing one body of Jesus Christ. Their hybrid identities, which are being built as one body by the transforming power of Jesus, thus help enhance their missional agency.

THE *LADINOS* AND FILIPINO AMERICAN PROTESTANTS

In the earlier part of this chapter, I argued that Filipino American Protestants are a contemporary form of the *ladinos*. In conclusion, I would like to highlight some overlapping points between these two groups of people.

117. Lee, *Marginality*, 170.
118. Walls, *Cross-cultural Process*, 76–81.

First, American Filipino Protestants, like the *ladinos*, function as not only cultural brokers and cultural changers between American and Filipino cultures. This chapter presented their bilingual capability (English and national language), hybrid identity between two different cultures (American and Filipino), and transnationalism (the continuing connection with the homeland) as the key factors that enable them to act as cultural brokers and changers.

Second, most Filipino American Protestants, like the *ladinos*, do not come from the ruling class in the Philippines, according to my ethnographic interviews. However, in the United States they have been promoted to the equivalent level of upper-middle or upper class in the Philippines in terms of economic power, education, and social status through their professional careers and networks. Noticeably, some of my interviewees still hold dual citizenships so that their promotions in status directly reflect some structural changes in the Philippines.

Third, Filipino American Protestants have impacted lives in the Philippines so that they trigger some tangible structural changes in the homeland. Filipino American Protestants have been helping in the economic growth of their families remaining in the Philippines, involved in political elections through their familial ties or their dual citizenships, supporting their siblings and relatives to get educated, which means providing them the most influential power sources. Consequently, they have helped people in the Philippines to be empowered, overcome a sense of powerless, and be promoted to a better status in society. They contribute to structural changes in the Philippines. In a similar way, the *ladino* class sourced their paradigms and tools from outside the indigenous culture.[119]

Fourth, Filipino Americans like the *ladinos* have sought structural changes for the Philippines through organizational power. In the case of the *ladinos,* they also contributed to structural changes in the Philippines through participating in the Propaganda Movement for reform against Spanish abuses and oppression.[120] This chapter describes how Filipino American Protestants have been helping reform the system of the Philippines through organizational networks from the United States to the Philippines.

Fifth, the only differences between American Filipino Protestants and the *ladinos* lie in their geographical location and religious orientation. While the *ladinos* lived inside the homeland, Filipino Americans live in the

119. Maggay, "Why the Poor," 19.
120. Mendoza, "Nuancing Anti-Essentialism," 236.

US. Whereas the *ladinos* were not motivated by any religious orientation for social change, Filipino American Protestants are inspired, motivated by their Protestant faith for the transformation of the Philippines (which is defined as missional agency in this chapter). Because of these differences, I named them a contemporary form of the *ladinos*. This chapter demonstrates how it is possible to bring about some crucial changes in power structures and social imaginaries through their missional agency. Although this seems to be incipient, this study revealed their great potentiality to transform the Philippines by presenting some successful cases.

In conclusion, Filipino American Protestants are a contemporary form of the *ladinos*. As they have been rarely spotlighted by academia as change agents for their homeland, this study unveiled their significant potentiality for the transformation of the Philippines.

CONCLUSION

As international migration became a common phenomenon in the world, Diaspora Missiology began to play a significant role in witnessing to the Gospel and planting new churches wherever *diaspora* go. *Diaspora* missions are a new strategy to fulfill the Great Commission in many places untouched by traditional missions. In this regard, the existence of Filipino American Protestants should be re-evaluated and their missional agency be more profoundly investigated with interest. To this purpose, in the earlier part of this chapter, I described the history of Filipino immigration to the United States in order to present who they are and why they move. I explained the major characteristics of Filipino American immigrants in comparison with the *ladinos* who were the culture brokers and culture changers throughout the Spanish and American colonial periods. In effect, Filipino American Protestants in my ethnographic research evidenced that they are wealthy, well-educated, professional in career, fluent both in Filipino and English, transnational and hybrid in identity by maintaining a continual connection with the homeland. I argued that their dual identity as Filipino and American not only fosters their flexibility and resiliency in adapting themselves to the United States, but also renders them able to embrace and reach out to other ethnic groups.

Furthermore, my interviewees testified that they have a strong calling from God to transform lives in the Philippines. I argued that their Protestant faith is missional and transformational in nature so that they are willing to commit themselves to achieving the Great Commandment in the

Philippines. To verify the missional agency of Filipino American Protestants, I presented seven different case studies on the basis of two models of Diaspora Missiology, that is, Mission *through* Diaspora and Mission *beyond* Diaspora. In light of Diaspora Missiology, Filipino *diasporas* in the United States have been placed by God for fulfilling the Great Commission and equipped and utilized by God as change agents for transforming a sense of powerlessness in their homeland.

6

Conclusion: Go Beyond the *Ladinos*

THIS STUDY CALLS ATTENTION to the sense of powerlessness of everyday people in the Philippines, and to the missional agency of Filipino American Protestants for the transformation of the Philippines. This study has been a journey to discover what kind of power is in play, how the fallen powers can be named and made visible, and then ultimately the ways through which power should be restored. In this process, I referred to the voices, perceptions, stories, and insights of Filipino American Protestants, in order to explore the causes of powerlessness because I posited that the solutions should be sought first within the causes of the problems.

Throughout the literature review and ethnographic research, I detected two major causes of powerlessness in the context of the Philippines: structural evil and social imaginaries. These two causes should be investigated and underscored more deeply so that everyday people will be aware of what takes place in everyday life in terms of power and how to prevent, overcome and even transform a sense of powerlessness. Furthermore, in this study Filipino American Protestants were investigated as the potential change agents for the transformation. The following section describes the findings of this study by answering the research questions.

FINDINGS

Research Question 1: How do US-based Filipino Protestants in Texas perceive and understand power structures in the Philippines? What do they think gives power?

First, this study revealed that the asymmetric structure of political-economic power in the Philippines causes and perpetuates a sense of powerlessness in everyday people with a lower socio-political-economic status. They face inequitable distribution of resources, believing that powerful outsiders are in control and, therefore, they cannot change anything by themselves to improve their situations.

Second, in the eyes of Filipino American Protestants, power can be both good and bad because it depends on how it is used. Whereas, for many participants in my interviews, power is good because it enables them to achieve what they want to do, some expressed displeasure toward the word *power* itself.

Third, in my ethnographic research with 31 participants, the most influential power source turned out to be money (18 out of 31 participants chose money), political position (6), education (4), family background (2), voice-out (1). However, when participants were given the chance to choose multiple factors, 15 participants, or 48.3 percent of all the participants, mentioned education as one of the most powerful factors that give people power.

Fourth, this study shows that the most powerful people in the context of the Philippines are politicians, the elite families, those who have money, and even religious leaders. Moreover, the most influential power sources in the Philippines are three: money, political position, and education. Noticeably, many of the participants tend to identify the word *power* with political leaders with some negative connotations because political leaders in the Philippines are notorious for corruption and self-interest.

Fifth, power structures in the Philippines are, in general, described as having the characteristics of power-over, such as hierarchical, oppressive, and coercive, particularly due to their own experiences, such as colonial history, rampant corruption of political leaders, dictatorship, pandemic poverty, and unequal opportunities.

Sixth, power structures in the Philippines cannot be explained without mentioning the patron-client relationship and elite families. In general, these elite families tend to be depicted as a root cause of oppressive

politics, eventually bringing about and perpetuating the structural inequality and injustice of Philippine society. The patron-client system of
pre-Hispanic times functioned positively in such a way that the leader
(patron) took care of his followers (clients) by offering them provisions
and protection. Throughout the Spanish colonial era, however, land-
based economics dominated by elite families of the colonizer birthed and
buttressed the patron-client system and ended up with oppressive politics
of the oligarchy up to today and the exploitative economics dominated by
a few elite families. In sum, the Philippines has a patrimonial oligarchic
state, meaning that a weak state is preyed upon a powerful oligarchy and
money has become a systemic product controlled by a powerful oligarchy
throughout Filipino history.

Seventh, this study revealed that everyday people in the context
of the Philippines depict religious leaders as among the greedy and
self-interested powerful elites. In the view of everyday people, religion,
particularly Roman Catholicism, has played a role in buttressing and perpetuating oppressive politics (the patron-client system, and the oligarchy) and exploitative economics (neo-patrimonial booty capitalism) in
the Philippines. Traditionally during the colonial period, religious leaders
were under patronage of the powerful. Even today, religious leaders are
often requested to say a blessing of prayer for those in powerful positions,
and are tempted to associate with them, not to provide moral guidance
but to obtain their own benefits.

Eighth, extraversion is another factor sustaining structural evil.
Throughout the colonial period and even nowadays, political leaders have
tried to compensate for difficulties in the country with the help of exterior
powers like colonizers, and today the United States. As a result, extraversion
brought about colonial mentality, colorism, preference for English, political
dependency, and economic exploitation. Concurrently, this study also suggested that extraversion is a tool used by everyday people on the ground to
circumvent the powers, and even change the structures. The Filipino American diaspora is one of the many outcomes of extraversion.

*Research Question 2: What Filipino cultural values or worldviews
do US-based Filipino Protestants in Texas view as causing and
perpetuating a sense of powerlessness in the Philippines?*

First, this study found that powerlessness is caused and perpetuated by
some cultural values in relation to social imaginaries. This study has

assessed that powerlessness is embedded in *Bahala na* and *Utang na loob* and everyday people in the Philippines use these cultural expressions which function at some mythic level in relation to social imaginaries that cause and perpetuate powerlessness.

Second, this study suggested that social imaginary has been birthed, nurtured, and eventually embedded in socio-political-economic structures. Structure and social imaginary, in this regard, are interconnected and influenced by one another. Asymmetric power structures make people powerless; concurrently under these structures social imaginaries are shaped, are nurtured, and gain legitimacy.

Third, my ethnographic research discovered that *Bahala na* tends to be recognized more as a fatalistic expression rather than agential. When people are confronted with challenging situations and hardship that are beyond their control, they utter this expression and consequently feed upon the powerlessness of everyday people in the Philippines.

Fourth, this study unveiled four religious soils embedded in *Bahala na,* which birthed, nurtured, and established a fatalistic bent in *Bahala na*: animism, Hinduism, Islam, and Catholicism. Particularly in the discussion of the influence of Catholicism on fatalism, some scholarly writings pointed out some plausible connections of fatalism between *Bahala na* and "Thy will be done" in the Lord's Prayer, which is regarded as a syncretistic form of Christianity.

Fifth, however, my interviews found that Filipino American Protestants in Texas do not utter *Bahala na* and they do not believe in destiny or fatalism. Moreover, to them the phrase "Thy Kingdom come" is not associated at all with a fatalistic meaning. Rather, they view God as the One who helps those who help themselves. Two factors accounted for this difference: their perspective in interpreting God's will and the awareness of agency in them. As mentioned in chapter 4, they may use *Bahala na* as an expression of leaving everything to God after doing their best. In discussing *Bahala na,* many of them mentioned God as the greatest helper in their lives, through whom they can do everything. Moreover, to contemporary Filipinos, it does not seem that *Bahala na* is directly perceived as a religious expression. Nevertheless, when they were asked to explain the meaning of this expression, they still seemed to unconsciously point to its religious connotation in such a way that many of them indirectly articulated how their lives had been empowered by the power of God.

They were convinced of spiritual power as their major power source for overcoming a sense of powerlessness.

Sixth, this study discovered that *Utang na loob* particularly in the asymmetric relationship between the beneficiary and benefactor can used at some mythic level in relation to a social imaginary triggering and perpetuating a sense of powerlessness. However, most of the interviewees concurred that *Utang na loob* is basically supposed to be a good cultural value facilitating interpersonal solidarity development, and generosity in times of need among the relationships.

Seventh, throughout my ethnographic research, I found that Filipino American Protestants in Texas do not practice *Utang na loob* in the church, even though it is still practiced by many others in the Filipino American communities where Filipino culture is more dominantly practiced and a Christian understanding of power is not articulated very much. Filipino American Protestants tend to practice this cultural value in a positive way to help someone in need. They do not expect their favor's return from the recipient, but rather help people because of the love and grace of Jesus. To them, *Utang na loob* is used as a tool to reinforce a Christian practice of unconditional reciprocal love. In other words, they took from their cultural heritage, but appropriate this cultural expression in a new way to give them agency and eventually transform the downside of *Utang na loob* through their spiritual discipline and the power of the Holy Spirit.

Research Question 3: How do US-based Filipino Protestants in Texas perceive, negotiate, and exercise power? How do they respond to their missional calling to transform lives in the Philippines?

First, to understand who Filipino American Protestants are, this study found out Filipino immigration to the United States, in general, has four phases: 1) during Spanish rule (the 16th century); 2) during the American colonization from 1900 to 1945; 3) during Post-Independence from 1946 to 1965; and 4) Post-Immigration and Nationality Act of 1965 from 1965 to 2000. I added a fifth phase to them: 5) 2001 to Present. Most new arrivals from the Philippines to the US are professionals, such as nurses, doctors, medical technologists, teachers, and the like. In addition, my ethnographic research testified to the contemporary trend that many families and relatives of Filipino immigrants continue to be invited to move to the US for the reunification of families.

Second, this study articulated the phenomenon of Filipinos-on-the-move as one consequential phenomenon representing the pervasiveness of powerlessness deeply rooted in the Philippines. Every year over a million temporary workers leave the Philippines to work overseas in more than 190 countries. Most of the participants in my ethnographic research testified to the reasons for leaving their home country to migrate to the United States: high poverty levels, joblessness, high underemployment rates, and political instability.

Third, my research unveiled that Filipino American immigrants in Texas are highly empowered. From the perspective of agency theory, they exercise agency at the high level of personal efficacy. Among participants in my ethnographic research, 13 out of 31 or more than 40 percent (41.9 percent) work in the medical field. Moreover, 9 of 16 female participants or 56.25 percent of them work in the medical field. This information verifies the literatures that include general information on Filipino Americans.

Fourth, as described in the previous section (Research Question 2), Filipino American Protestants have negotiated, modified, and complemented a sense of powerlessness embedded in Filipino cultural values, not only because of their practice of power based upon Protestant faith but also by their highly developed individual agency through education, wealth, professional career, and their American way of living and thinking.

Fifth, Filipino American Protestants are transnational and hybrid in identity. They continue to have contact with home in the Philippines, by sending numerous *balikbayan boxes* or care packages of assorted goods and remittances on a regular basis, by watching Filipino news and TV shows, by participating in political elections through their familial networks,[1] and by engaging in civic movements via organizations. In this process, they belong to more than one world, speak more than one language, and inhabit more than one identity. They constantly construct and re-construct their homeland and Filipino *diaspora* community in the United States. In light of agency theory, they exercise their proxy agency, which means they act on behalf of Filipino families in the Philippines especially for financial support. They also exercise their collective agency by establishing some organizations to help and transform the lives in the Philippines. Based on the research, I came to this conclusion: their

1. In my ethnographic research, I found that some of them hold dual citizenship so that they are able to vote for political election directly in the Philippines; others hold only American citizenship so that they can impact the political elections in the Philippines through their familial networks.

hybridity in identity and transnationalism have granted flexibility and resiliency to Filipino immigrants between different cultures throughout the history of Spanish rule and American colonization, and even nowadays their international migration in the globalized world.

Sixth, in this regard, I argued that Filipino American Protestants are the contemporary form of the *ladinos* who brought about some alternative changes in power structures and social imaginaries in the Philippines. The potentiality of Filipino American Protestants as the change agents centers on their bilingual capability between English and Filipino (Tagalog), high economic-educational status, professional careers, differentiated perception on power due to Protestantism, continuing connection with the mainland Philippines through some familial ties and organizational networks, and consequent hybrid identity between two different cultures (American and Filipino). The only differences between Filipino American Protestants and the *ladinos* lie in geographical location and the religious orientation. While the *ladinos* lived inside the homeland, Filipino Americans live in the United States. Whereas the *ladinos* were not motivated by any religious orientation for social change, Filipino American Protestants are inspired, motivated by their Protestant faith for the transformation of the Philippines.

Seventh, throughout my ethnographic research, I discovered that their Protestant faith is the major resource to inspire them to strongly believe in the transformation of the Philippines, to motivate them to participate in the Great Commandment to transform the people. Moreover, their Protestant faith manifested in Diaspora Missiology gives them assurance that their migration to the United States has missiological meaning in the eyes of God to fulfill God's missions through them.

Eighth, in this study, I defined missional agency as the capability of Christians as individuals and the Church as a whole to intentionally make their own free choice of participating in God's mission regardless of external constraints, in order to explain their religious aspiration for transformation and to describe some potential changes triggered by them with respect to a sense of powerlessness in the Philippines.

Ninth, this study analyzed the missional agency of Filipino American Protestants through some case studies in light of Diaspora Missiology, that is, mission *through* diasporas and mission *by* and *beyond* diasporas. For the model of mission *through* diasporas, I presented four different case studies: empowering Filipinos through education, spiritual transformation through raising spiritual leaders, sending rescue mission teams to the Philippines, and networking with other organization to impact the Philippines. For the model of mission *by* and *beyond* diasporas, three case studies were depicted: church and a community center, church reaching out to other ethnic groups locally and globally, church embracing a Hispanic congregation as their church family.

Tenth, this study revealed that in the discourse of transformation in the Philippines, Filipino American Protestants tend to be reminded of corruption as the major target to be transformed. For many of them, bringing about transformation means putting a spiritual man of integrity and sincerity into political position, one who is not tempted to be corrupt and who is expected to transform the corruptive power structures. According to my interviewees, for getting this change to take place, there should be a spiritual awakening in the hearts of people, which is only possible through the transforming power of God. For this reason, they want to take part in educating spiritual leaders in the Philippines by sending scholarships, and supporting seminaries. Thus, they understand that transformation of the Philippines through individuals' spiritual transformation should result in structural transformation. I think that their perception on transformation came from their conservative theology instilled and shaped by some conservative American Protestant missionaries. Moreover, some of this perspective might also come from their experience with American life where American Evangelicals tend to interpret change through the personal integrity of a leader. In sum, although their perception on transformation has part of the truth, unless complemented holistically, it seems to fall into reductionism. Transformation has to take place in such a holistic way of not only bringing individuals to Christ but also challenging corrupt and sinful systems, structures and cultures so that everyday people and communities will be able to experience God's transforming power. Noticeably, in the model of mission *through* diaspora, one case study of networking with other organization to impact the Philippines described the high potentiality that Filipino American diasporas can exercise their missional agency in the form of power-with, that is through organizational networking by suggesting that the Philippine government reform some crucial policies regarding politics, economics, and the like. This kind of model is incipient, and needs to be more developed for a holistic understanding of transformation in the Philippines.

Eleventh, this study revealed that they exercise not only individual agency at the high level, but also collective agency as a group. I argued that Filipino American Protestants would need to be more spotlighted in terms of their collective agency as change agents for the transformation of the Philippines.

Research Question 4: What theological meanings do US-based Filipino Protestants in Texas give to power?

Throughout the ethnographic research, I found out that Filipino American Protestants are keen to recognize the existence of social structures and interpret cultural values based on biblical teachings. Not only that, in effect many of them understand and practice power theologically. One participant said that he feels more powerful when he gets closer to the Lord. To him, power seems to be more of a spiritual power.

Nevertheless, only one third of my interviewees or 10 out of 31 were able to answer my research question, "What theological meanings do Filipino American Protestants give to power?"

Four participants designated the image of God (Genesis 1:26) as the original source of power, whereby all kinds of human beings regardless of being the rich, the poor, the powerless, and the powerful are equally given power from God. Although the concept of the *Kenosis* of Jesus was not directly articulated, some interviewees described Jesus as the biblical example of how to use power: Jesus' servant leadership in washing the feet of His disciples, being born humbly in a manger, being obedient to death on the cross to save us. One interviewee mentioned 2 Corinthian 12:9 to explain that God's power is made perfect in weakness. Throughout the ethnographic interviews, the concept of The Trinity was not mentioned at all. The Trinitarian understanding of power, however, is the very essence of relational power based upon God's attributes (particularly love), which is highlighted in the Bible. Four participants explained power in the similar ways: "Ultimately it is God who has power"; "God is in control and leads everything"; "I can do all this through him who gives me strength (Philippians 4:13)." However, in these ways God is seen as the Patron, and believers are the clients. Their perception on power seems to be based on power-over. Therefore, it needs to be complemented by other forms of power like power-to and power-within. Furthermore, the omnipotence or absolute power of God should be accompanied by the *Kenosis* of Jesus to avoid justifying the church's compromise with the worldly powers.

I strongly recommend Filipino American Protestant Churches to develop their own theology of power and teach it to everyday people so that the church will be able to enhance and maintain their missional agency more effectively.

GO BEYOND THE *LADINOS*

In this study, I argued that Filipino American Protestants are the contemporary form of the *ladinos*. In chapter 5, I highlighted some overlapping points between these two groups of people. First of all, Filipino American Protestants, like the *ladinos*, function as cultural brokers and cultural changers. The major characteristics enabling this are their transnationalism (continual connection with homeland), hybrid identity (flexibility and resiliency) between two different cultures (American and Filipino), bilingual capability (English and national language), higher educational-economic attainment, and professional careers. On top of that, the promotions in status of both Filipino American Protestants and the *ladinos* directly or indirectly reflect some structural changes in the Philippines. Moreover, as the *ladino* class sourced their paradigms and tools from outside the indigenous culture,[2] Filipino American Protestants, according to chapter 5, have been of great help as power resources to their families, relatives, and other Christians. Further, Filipino American Protestants, like what the *ladinos* did through the Propaganda Movement, contribute to structural changes in the Philippines through organizational networks from the United States to the Philippines.

What then makes Filipino American Protestants go beyond the *ladinos*? I argue it is their missional agency, that is, their spiritual commitment to believe in the transforming power of God and willingness to become the divine vessel for transformation. Whereas the *ladinos* were not motivated by any religious orientation for social change, Filipino American Protestants are inspired, motivated by their Protestant faith for transformation of the Philippines. In light of the Transformational Development and Public Theology underlying the entire study as its Theoretical Framework, I presented how they perceive, negotiate, and transform a sense of power through their spiritual discipline and Protestant faith. Chapter 4 showcased how US-based Filipino Protestants in Texas had brought about the transformation of a sense of powerlessness embedded in Filipino cultural practices like *Bahala na* and *Utang na loob*. In this sense, they are already living beyond the *ladinos*. In addition, seven case studies in chapter 5 showcased how US-based Filipino Protestants had engaged in public issues of the

2. Maggay, "Why the Poor," 19.

Philippines to transform the structural evil through some organizational networks such as FAITH (Filipino-American Initiative to Transform our Homeland), US Pinoy 4 Good Governance, and continuing ecclesiastical networks with local churches and seminaries in the Philippines. Despite these positive achievements of US-based Filipino Protestants, I have to admit that their missional agency is still incipient, and should be more developed in the future. Hopefully, this study will be a milestone on which they will not only continue to find and desire God's calling as agents of transformation, but also cultivate, and develop their missional agency in them (individual agency) and among them (collective agency).

MISSIOLOGICAL IMPLICATIONS

Five missiological implications from this study are as follows:

First, a sense of powerlessness should be understood in a holistic way. Some people argue that attitude and mentality matter most. However, Walter Wink reminds us, "Powerlessness is not simply a problem of attitude . . . There are structures—economic, political, religious, and only then psychological—that oppress people and resist all attempts to end their oppression."[3] We should not ignore the disempowering influences of structural evil. For this reason, as introduced in chapter 1, transformation has to take place holistically, not only bringing individuals to Christ but also challenging corrupt and sinful systems, structures and cultures so that everyday people and communities will be able to experience God's transforming power. In this study, I explored structural evil embedded in socio-political-economic systems in the Philippines first and then moved on to deal with the attitude and mentality of everyday people with special reference to a sense of powerlessness.

Second, sociological methods used in this study offers crucial insight into how to observe, interpret, and analyze the context of "a peculiar Sitz im Leben"[4] or situation in life of everyday people in the Philippines. To understand the structural evil and social imaginaries embedded in "situation in life" of everyday people is the very starting point to seek after the transformation of a sense of powerlessness. Therefore, "theology and sociology need to deepen dialogue with each other" because "sociological methods provide essential insight into *how* (and *why*) ecclesiastical agents think about theologically nuanced subjects, underscoring the importance of context in the

3. Wink, *Engaging the Powers*, 102.
4. Bosh, *Transforming Mission*, 422.

hermeneutical process."[5] Without understanding the dynamics of power in a society, we cannot bring a long-term change. For this purpose, a deeper dialogue between theology and sociology needs to be developed by the Filipino Protestant Church in the Philippines.

Third, this study illuminates the significance of a theological understanding of power. A theology of power unveils the roots of fallen human beings and their fallen social structures and provides the ethical and spiritual criteria to the fallen world. The task of theology and religion, according to Max L. Stackhouse, is "provide a reasonable proposal with regard to the moral and spiritual architecture and the inner guidance systems of civilization."[6] The invisible culture is more powerful and the invisible power is more powerful. For long-term social change, we have to not only change forms, but also largely talk about values, meanings that undergird the outer forms at the same time. Once powerlessness is deeply embedded as a form of culture, it is apt to become part of the identity of people and then hard to change because people uncritically absorb it, and practice it unintentionally. This is what Paul Germond means: "As long as our identities are shaped reflexively, as long as power is exercised unintentionally, then we are incarnated by it, molded by its contours in ways of which we are not remotely aware."[7] For this reason, this study has intentionally investigated and critically analyzed some cultural values to reveal the focal points where transformation should take place. Particularly, I sketched some religious soils of a Filipino cultural value like *Bahala na*. According to Peter Berger, the religious beliefs and meanings held by individuals construct "plausibility structures," in which the members of a society legitimate social practices and orders.[8] In this regard, I believe that a theological understanding of power provides the platform on which a sense of powerlessness can be perceived, analyzed, and eventually transformed. Nevertheless, the church's theological discourse on power should not be justification for ignoring the need to work for the actual transformation of the power structures in the world.

Fourth, this study encourages the churches' engagement in the public arena. As demonstrated in chapter 5, Filipino American Protestants have utilized the networks of other individual denominations, local churches,

---

5. Okession, *Re-Imaging Modernity*, 222.

6. Stackhouse, *Globalization and Grace*, 84.

7. Germond, "Theology, Development, and Power," 30.

8. Berger, *Sacred Canopy*, 48.

and organizations to make use of their intentional and relational dimensions of power in the public arena of the Philippines. The Church has to recognize that "their identities as social beings and social actors profoundly influence the way in which they regard themselves in the world and construct their sense of agency."[9]

Fifth, this study investigated and analyzed the missional agency of Filipino American Protestants who have been rarely spotlighted as change agents for the Philippines in the academia of missiology and intercultural studies. Noticeably, this study unveiled not only their individual agency but also their collective agency as a group by presenting seven case studies. This is where this study can contribute to the literature.

LIMITATIONS AND RECOMMENDATIONS FOR FURTHER STUDY

To conclude this study, I describe here the limitations of this study and make some recommendations for further study on the issue of powerlessness.

First, for further research, powerlessness should be studied from the eyes of Filipinos living in the Philippines. The major causes for powerlessness explored with the eyes of Filipino American Protestants need to be examined by Filipino Protestants in the Philippines. Then, a comparison of the data collected from the Philippines with those from this study should be made in terms of how similar and different they are.

Second, to research is needed on cultural values that might possibly give people a sense of power, instead of powerlessness, and enable them to survive poverty in the Philippines. Here are some potential values: *pakka-pamilya* or close emotional ties and reciprocal obligations to family and *pakikipag-kapwa* or human concern and interaction with others.[10]

Third, further study would be ideal on the missional agency of Filipino Protestants in the Philippines with some cases for transformational development in the Philippines. This study explored Filipino American Protestants and change agents for the Philippines. However, there is also much potential among Filipino Protestants for transforming the Philippines. Practical examples that actualize the theory will buttress the validity of the theory.

9. Germond, "Theology, Development, and Power," 22.
10. Tuason, "Those Who Were Born Poor," 52.

Fourth, missional agency of Filipino American Protestants needs to be reviewed by Filipino Protestants in the Philippines. Although this study highlighted Filipino diasporas in the United States, I am curious how this study will be read and understood by Filipino Protestants in the homeland. Some people in the Philippines might argue that Filipino American Protestants' missional agency is not felt at all. Some other people might say that they do need to partner with Filipino American Protestants for the transformation of the Philippines. In this process, research should also explore how these two different groups of people perceive each other in terms of power.

Fifth, it will be interesting to compare the data collected from the eyes of Filipino American Protestants in Texas with some other different cases in cities bigger than those in Texas, where there are more Filipinos in number and bigger Filipino communities in size. One interviewee gave a hint at this: "If you put more mice in a cage, the more mice you put in one cage, the more aggressive they tend to be." A sense of powerlessness among Filipino Americans in the bigger cities will be an interesting topic to be explored.

Bibliography

Adams, Suzi, et al. "Social Imaginaries in Debate." *Social Imaginaries* 1 (2015) 15–52.

Agoncillo, Teodoro A. "Filipino Traits and Custom." http://web.archive.org/web/200604 19070300/www.rogersantos.org/filtraits.html.

Agunias, Dovelyn. *Linking Temporary Worker Schemes with Development*. Washington, DC: Migration Policy Institute, 2007.

Allen, Vernon L., ed. *Psychological Factors in Poverty*. Chicago: Markham, 1970.

Anderson, Benedict. "Cacique Democracy in the Philippines: Origins and Dreams." *New Left Review* 169 (1988) 3–31.

———. *Imagined Communities*. Verso, 1991.

Andres, T. D. *Dictionary of Filipino Culture and Values*. Quezon City, the Philippines: Giraffe, 1994.

Appadurai, Arjun. *Modernity at Large*. Minneapolis: University of Minnesota Press, 1996.

Arendt, Hannah. *The Human Condition*. Chicago: University of Chicago Press, 1958.

———. "On Violence." In *Cries of the Republic*, 103–84. New York and London: Harcourt Brace Jovanovich, 1969.

Arthurs, Alberta. "Social Imaginaries and Global Realities." *Public Culture* 15 (2003) 579–86.

Baker, Chris. *Cultural Studies: Theory and Practice*. London: Sage, 2005.

Barth, Karl. *Church Dogmatics, Volume 3: The Doctrine of Creation, part 1: The Work of Creation*. Edinburgh: Clark, 1958.

Bayart, Jean-François "Africa in the World: A History of Extraversion." *African Affairs* (2000) 217–67.

Bedford-Strohm, Heinrich. "Tilling and Caring for the Earth: Public Theology and Ecology." *International Journal of Public Theology* 1 (2007) 230–48.

Bello, Walden, and John Gershman. "Democratization and Stabilization in the Philippines." *Critical Sociology* 17 (1990) 35–56.

Berger, Peter. *The Sacred Canopy*. New York: Doubleday & Company, 1967.

Blommaert, Jan, and Dong Jie. *Ethnographic Fieldwork*. New York: Multilingual Matters, 2010.

Bosh, David J. *Transforming Mission*. New York: Orbis, 1991.

Bibliography

Bostrom, Lynn C. "Filipino *Bahala na* and American Fatalism." *Silliman Journal* 15 (1968) 399–413.

Brady, Marilyn Dell. *The Asian Texans*. College Station, TX: Texas A&M University Press, 2004.

Brueggemann, Walter. *The Prophetic Imagination*. Minneapolis: Fortress, 2001.

Buckles, Jeffrey J. "What Are the Educational Implications of Developing a New Social Imaginary, Brought about by the Challenges to be Faced in the 21st Century?" PhD diss., University of Hull, 2015.

Bulatao, Jaime. *Split-Level Christianity*. Philippines: Ateneo De Manila University, 1966.

———. "Split-Level Christianity." *Philippines Sociological Review* 13 (1965) 119–21.

Cartagenas, Aloysius Lopez. "Religion and Politics in the Philippines: The Public Role of the Roman Catholic Church in the Democratization of the Filipino Polity." *Political Theology* 11 (2010) 846–72.

Casiño, Tereso C. "Mission in the Context of Filipino Folk Spirituality: *Bahala na* as a Case in Point." *Seoul Consultation, Study Commission IX*. Edinburgh: n.d., 2010.

Castoriadis, Cornelius. *The Imaginary Institution of Society*. Cambridge, MA: MIT University Press, 1987.

Catalan, Daisy C. S. "The Diversity of the Filipinos in the United States." http://teachersinstitute.yale.edu/curriculum/units/1996/4/96.04.05.x.html.

Chambers, Robert. *Rural Development: Putting the Last First*. London: Longman, 1983.

Cherry, Stephen M. *Faith, Family, and Filipino American Community Life*. New Brunswick, NJ: Rutgers University Press, 2014.

Chester, Tim, ed. *Justice, Mercy, and Humility: Integral Mission and the Poor*. Carlisle, UK: Paternoster, 2002.

Christian, Jayakumar. *"Powerlessness of the Poor: Toward an Alternative Kingdom of God Paradigm of Response."* PhD diss., Fuller Theological Seminary, 1994.

Clement, Luis F. *"Running Head: Colonial Mentality and Anxiety in Filipino Americans."* PsyD diss., The California School of Professional Psychology at Alliant International University, 2014.

Constantino, Renato. *Dissent and Counter-consciousness*. Manila: Erehwon, 1970

Cordova, Fred. *Filipinos: Forgotten Asian Americans: a pictorial essay*. Dubuque, IA: Kendal/Hunt, 1983.

Corpuz, Onofre D. *The Philippines*. Eaglewood Cliffs, NJ: Prentice-Hall, 1965.

Crane, Julia G. and Michael V. Angrosino. *Field Projects in Anthropology*. Love Grove, IL: Waveland, 1992.

Davao City Ministerial Fellowship on June 13, 2011. http://waves.ca/2011/06/14/description-of-the-evangelical-church-today/.

David, E. J. R. "Cultural Mistrust and Help-Seeking Attitudes." *Asian American Journal of Psychology* 1 (2010) 57–66.

David, E. J. R., and Sumie Okazaki. "The Colonial Mentality Scale for Filipino Americans: Scale Construction and Psychological Implications." *Journal of Counseling Psychology* (2006) 1–16.

———. "Colonial Mentality: A Review and Recommendation for Filipino American Psychology." *Cultural Diversity and Ethnic Minority Psychology* 12 (2006) 1–16.

De Mesa, José M. *And God Said, "Bahala na!": The Theme of Providence in the Lowland Filipino Context*. Quezon City, the Philippines: Publishers' Printing, 1979.

———. *In Solidarity with Culture: Studies in Theological Re-Rooting*. Quezon City, the Philippines: Maryhill School of Theology, 1987.

Dictionary.com. "Colonialism." http://www.dictionary.com/browse/colonialism.

Diokno, Maria Serena I. "The Democratising Function of Citizenship in the Philippines." In *Globalisation and Citizenship in the Asia Pacific*, edited by Alastair Davidson and Kathleen Weekly 134–54. Basingstoke: Macmillan, 1999.

Dillistone, Frederick W. *The Structure of the Divine Society*. Philadelphia: Westminister, 1951.

Doronila, Amando. "The Transformation of Patron-Client Relations and Its Political Consequences in Postwar Philippines." *Journal of Southeast Asian Studies* 16 (1985) 99–116.

Downey, Michael. *Altogether Gift: A Trinitarian Spirituality*. Maryknoll, NY: Orbis, 2000.

Emerson, Michael O., and Karen Chai Kim. "Multicultural Congregation: An Analysis of Their Development and a Typology." *Journal for Scientific Study of Religion* 42 (2003) 217–27.

Encyclopedia Britannica. "Anthony-Giddens." https://www.britannica.com/biography/Anthony-Giddens.

———. "Hannah Arendt." https://www.britannica.com/biography/Hannah-Arendt.

———. "Karl-Marx." https://www.britannica.com/biography/Karl-Marx.

———. "Max Weber." https://www.britannica.com/biography/Max-Weber-German-sociologist.

———. "Michel Foucault." https://www.britannica.com/biography/Michel-Foucault.

Eriksen, Thomas Hylland. *Ethnicity and Nationalism*. London: Pluto, 2002.

Espiritu, Yen Le. *Home Bound*. Los Angeles: University of California Press, 2003.

Fifteenth Census of The United States 1930. "Table 20.—Population of the Minor Races Other Than Mexican, By Nativity, By States: 1930, 1920, and 1910-Continued." In *Population Volume II: General Report Statistics by Subjects*. Washington, DC: United States Government Printing Office, 1933.

Foucault, Michel. *Power/Knowledge: Selected Interviews and Other Writings 1972–1977*, edited by *Colin Gordon*. New York: Pantheon, *1980*.

Ferguson, Kathy E. *The Feminist Case Against Bureaucracy*. Philadelphia: Temple University Press, 1984.

Fernandez, Eleazar. "Exodus-toward-Egypt: Filipino-Americans' Struggle to Realize the Promised Land in America." In *A Dream Unfinished: Theological Reflections on America from the Margins*, edited by Fernando Segovia and Eleazer Fernandez, 167–84. Maryknoll, NY: Orbis, 2001.

Francia, Luis H. *A History of the Philippines: From Indios Bravos to Filipinos*. New York: The Overlook, 2010.

Friedmann, John. *Empowerment: The Politics of Alternative Development*. Cambridge, MA: Blackwell, 1992.

Gallery of Texas Cultures. "Filipino Texans." University of Texas at Austin. http://texascultures.housing.utexas.edu/assets/pdfs/GTC_filipinotexans.pdf.

Gardner, Andrew. *Agency Uncovered*. New York: Routledge, 2016.

Gerard, Clarke, and Marites Sison. "Voices from the Top of the Pile: Elite Perceptions of Poverty and the Poor in the Philippines." *Development and Change* 34 (2003) 215–42.

Germond, Paul. "Theology, Development, and Power." *Journal of Theology for Southern Africa* 110 (2001) 41–69.

Giddens, Anthony. *The Constitution of Society: Outline of the Theory of Structuration*. Berkley: University of California Press, 1984.

Bibliography

———. *A Contemporary Critique of Historical Materialism*. Berkley: University of California Press, 1981.

———. "On the Relation of Sociology to Philosophy." In *Explaining Human Behavior: Consciousness, Human Action, and Social Structure*. Beverly Hills, CA: Sage, 1982.

———. *Profiles and Critiques in Social Theory*. Berkley: University of California Press, 1982.

———. "Remarks on the Theory of Power." In *Studies in Social and Political Theory*, 333–49. New York: Basic, 1977.

Gifford, Paul. *Christianity, Development, and Modernity in Africa*. New York: Oxford University Press, 2016.

Gorospe, Vitaliano R. "Understanding the Filipino Value System." In *Values in Philippine Culture and Education*, 63–70. Washington, DC: The Council for Research in Values and Philosophy, 1994.

Graham, Elaine. "A Window on the Soul: Four Politicians on Religion and Public Life." *International Journal of Public Theology* 3 (2009) 145–64.

Green, Duncan. *From Poverty to Power*. Oxford: Oxfam International, 2012.

Gripaldo, Rolando M. "Bahala na: A Philosophical Analysis." *Filipino Cultural Traits: Claro R. Ceniza Lectures. Council for Research in Values and Philosophy* (2005) 194–211.

———. *Filipino Cultural Traits: Claro R. Ceniza Lectures*, Washington, DC: Council for Research in Values and Philosophy, 2005.

Guerrero, Linda Luz. "Social Inequality in the Philippines: The 1992 ISSP survey." *SWS Occasional paper*. Manila: Social Weather Stations.

Gunton, Colin. *The Promise of the Trinity*. Edinburgh: T. & T. Clark, 1991.

Halili, Maria. *Philippine History*. Quezon City, the Philippines: Rex, 2010.

Hall, Stuart. "New Cultures for Old." In *A Place in the World? Places, Cultures, and Globalization*, edited by Doreen B. Massey and Pat Jess, 175–214. Oxford: Oxford University Press, 1995.

Hanciles, Jehu J. "Migration and Mission: The Religious Significance of the North-South Divide." In *Mission in the 21st Century*, edited by Andrew Walls and Cathy Ross. New York: Orbis, 2008.

Harris, Susan K. *God's Arbiters: Americans and the Philippines, 1898–1902*. Oxford: Oxford University Press, 2011.

Harrison, Lawrence E. *Underdevelopment is a State of Mind*. New York: Madison, 2000.

Hawes, Gary. *The Philippine State and the Marcos Regime: The Politics of Export*. Ithaca: Cornell University Press, 1987.

Hewson, Martin. "Agency." In *Encyclopedia of Case Study Research*, edited by Albert J. Mills et al. Thousand Oaks, CA: SAGE, 2010.

Hiebert, Paul G., et al. *Understanding Folk Religion: A Christian Response to Popular Beliefs and Practices*. Grand Rapids: Baker, 1999.

Hinze, Christine Firer. *Comprehending Power in Christian Social Ethics*. Atlanta: Scholars, 1995.

Hollnsteiner, Mary. *The Dynamics of Power in a Philippine Municipality*. Quezon City: University of the Philippines, 1963.

———. "Reciprocity in the Lowland Philippines." In *Four Readings on Philippine Values*, 69–92. Quezon City: Ateneo de Manila University Press, 1964.

Hughes, Dewi. *Power and Poverty*. Downers Grove, IL: InterVarsity, 2008.

Hunter, James Davison. *To Change the World: The Irony, Tragedy, and Possibility of Christianity in the Late Modern World*. New York: Oxford University Press, 2010.

Hutchcroft, Paul. *Booty Capitalism: The Politics of Banking in the Philippines*. Ithaca: Cornell University Press, 1998.

Inda, Jonathan Xavier, and Renato Rosaldo. "Tracking Global Flows." In *The Anthropology of Globalization*, 3–46. MA: Blackwell, 2008.

Inquirer.net. "Remittances of Overseas Filipino Workers." http://business.inquirer.net/233394/ofw-remittances-5-5-2-3b-may#ixzz50RO7FMa7.

Jayakaran, Ravi. *Participatory Learning and Action: User Guide and Mannual*. Madras, India: World Vision India, 1996.

Jenkins, Philip. *The Next Christendom*. New York: Oxford University Press: 2011.

Jocano, F. Landa. *Folk Christianity: A Preliminary Study of Conversion and Patterning of Christian Experience in the Philippines*. Quezon City, the Philippines: Trinity Research Institute, 1981.

Karnow, Stanley. *In Our Image: America's Empire in the Philippines*. New York: Ballantine, 1990.

Kaut, C. R. "Utang na loob: A System of Contractual Obligation." *Southwestern Journal of Anthropology* 17 (1961) 256–72.

Kerkvliet, Benedict. "Toward a More Comprehensive Analysis of Philippine Politics: Beyond the Patron-Client, Factional Framework." *Journal of Southeast Asian Studies* 26 (1995) 401–19.

Kierkegaard, Søren. *Christian Discourses*. Edited and translated by Howard V. Hong and Edna H. Hong. Princeton: Princeton University Press, 1997.

King, Martin Luther, Jr. "Where Do We Go From Here?" Annual Report Delivered at the 11th Convention of the Southern Christian Leadership Conference, August 16, 1967, in Atlanta, GA. http://www-personal.umich.edu/~gmarkus/MLK_WhereDoWeGo.pdf.

LA Weekend Asian Journal. August 1–4, 2015, C6. https://issuu.com/asianjournaldigitaledition/docs/la_weekend_august_01-04__2015/1.

Landé, Carl. *Leaders, Factions and Parties: The Structure of Philippines Politics*. New Haven, CT: Yale University Press, 1965

Lausanne Movement, "The Seoul Declaration on Diaspora Missiology." https://www.lausanne.org/content/statement/the-seoul-declaration-on-diaspora-missiology.

Lee, Jung Young. *Marginality: The Key to Multicultural Theology*. Minneapolis: Fortress, 1995.

Lewellen, Ted C. *The Anthropology of Globalization*. Westport, CT: Bergin and Garvey, 2002.

Lichauco, Alejandro. *The Lichauco Paper: Imperialism in the Philippines*. New York: Monthly Review, 1973.

Licuanan, Patricia B. "A Moral Recovery Program: Building a People—Building a Nation." In *Values in Philippine Culture and Education*, 35–54. Washington, DC: The Council for Research in Values and Philosophy, 1994.

Linthicum, Robert. *Transforming Power*. Downers Grove, IL: InterVarsity, 2003.

Maggay, Melba Padilla. "Why the Poor are Always with Us: A Filipino Christian's Propositions." *Ogbomoso Journal of Theology* 14 (2009) 17–35.

Marx, Karl. "Economic and Philosophic Manuscripts of 1844." In *The Marx-Engels Reader*, edited by Robert C. Tucker, 66–125. New York: W. W. Norton and Company, 1978.

Marx, Karl, and Friedrich Engels. *The Communist Manifesto*. Suwanee, GA: 12th Media Services, 2018.

Bibliography

Matheny, Paul D. "Ferment at the Margins: Philippines Ecclesiology Under Stress." *International Bulletin of Missionary Research* 35 (2011) 202–7.

McIntosh, Jason M. "Paradigm of Power and Authority in the Kingdom of God: A Study of the Utilization of Power and Authority and Congregational Health." DMin diss., Asbury Theological Seminary, 2009.

Mendoza, S. Lily. "Nuancing Anti-Essentialism: A Critical Genealogy of the Philippine Experiments in National Identity Formation." In *Between Law and Culture*, 244–45. Minneapolis: University of Minnesota Press, 2001.

Mercadal, Trudy. *Salem Press Encyclopedia*. Amenia, NY: Salem, 2014.

Mercado, Leonardo N. *Elements of Filipino Philosophy*. Tacloban City, the Philippines: Divine Word University, 1976.

Merriam-Webster Dictionary. "Clientelism." https://www.merriam-webster.com/dictionary/clientelism.

———. "Pensionado." https://www.merriam-webster.com/dictionary/pensionado.

Middleton, Richard J. *The Liberating Image: The Imago Dei in Genesis 1*. Grand Rapids: Brazos, 2005.

Migration Policy Institute (MPI). "Filipino Immigrants in the United States." https://www.migrationpolicy.org/article/filipino-immigrants-united-states.

———. "Largest Immigrant Groups." https://www.migrationpolicy.org/programs/data-hub/charts/largest-immigrant-groups-over-time.

———. "Linking Temporary Worker Schemes with Development." http://www.migrationpolicy.org/article/linking-temporary-worker-schemes-development.

Moltmann, Jürgen. *The Trinity and the Kingdom: The Doctrine of God*. San Francisco: Harper & Row, 1981.

Mommsen, Wolfgang. *The Age of Bureaucracy: Perspectives on the Political Sociology of Max Weber*. Oxford: Basil Blackwell, 1974.

Mott, Stephen C. *Biblical Ethics and Social Change*. New York: Oxford University Press, 2011.

Murchison, Julian M. *Ethnography Essentials: Designing, Conducting, and Presenting Your Research*. San Francisco: Jossey-Bass, 2010.

Muslimink.com. "In Allah We Trust: What *Tawakkul* Really Means." https://www.muslimink.com/islam/tawakkul/.

Musopole, A. C. "African World View." *Prepared for Changing the Story: Christian Witness and Transformational Development Consultation*. May 5–10, World Vision, Pasadena, CA.

Myers, Bryant L. *Walking with the poor: Principles and Practices of Transformational Development*. Maryknoll, NY: Orbis, 2011.

"National Statistics Office." http://webo.psa.gov.ph/sites/default/files/2014%20PIF.pdf.

"Negros Occidental Government." http://www.negros-occ.gov.ph/directory/municipality-officials-of-negros-occidental.

Office of the President of the Philippines. "Commission on Filipinos Overseas." http://www.cfo.gov.ph/news/cfo-news-and-events/77-us-pinoys-for-good-governance-usp4gg-fully-committed-to-the-motherland.html.

Offutt, Stephen, et. al. *Advocating for Justice: An Evangelical Vision for Transforming Systems and Structures*. Grand Rapids: Baker, 2016.

Okesson, Gregg A. *Re-Imaging Modernity: A Contextualized Theological Study of Power and Humanity within Akamba Christianity in Kenya*. Eugene, OR: Pickwick, 2012.

Oord, Thomas Jay. *Defining Love: A Philosophical, Scientific, and Theological Engagement.* Grand Rapids: Brazos, 2010.

Pal, Agaton P. "A Philippine Barrio." *University of Manila Journal of East Asiatic Studies* 5 (1965) 333–486.

Pedraza, Silvia, and Reuben G. Rumbaut, *Origins and Destinies: Immigration, Race, and Ethnicity in America.* Belmont, CA: Wadsworth, 1996.

Pe-Pua, Rogelia, and Elizabeth Protacio-Marcelino. "Sikolohiyang Pilipino (Filipino psychology): A Legacy of Virgilio G. Enriquez." *Asian Journal of Social Psychology* 3 (2000) 49–71.

Pew Research Center. "Asian Americans: A Mosaic of Faiths." http://www.pewforum.org /2012/07/19/asian-americans-a-mosaic-of-faiths-religious-affiliation/.

———. "Filipinos in the U.S. Fact Sheet." http://www.pewsocialtrends.org/fact-sheet/ asian-americans-filipinos-in-the-u-s/.

Philippine Statistics Authority. "Philippines in Figures: 2014, National Statistics Office." http://webo.psa.gov.ph/sites/default/files/2014%20PIF.pdf.

———. "Survey on Overseas Filipinos 2016." https://www.psa.gov.ph/content/2016-survey-overseas-filipinos.

"Philippines—History and Background." http://education.stateuniversity.com/ pages/1197/Philippines-HISTORY-BACKGROUND.html.

"Political and Economic Risk Consultancy, Ltd.-PERC." http://www.asiarisk.com/index. html.

Post, Stephen G. *Unlimited Love: Altruism, Compassion, and Service.* Philadelphia: Templeton Foundation, 2003.

Postma, Antoon. "The Laguna Copper-Plate Inscription: Text and Commentary." *Philippine Studies* 40 (1992) 183–203.

Prilleltensky, Issac. "Poverty and Power." In *Poverty and Psychology: From Global Perspective to Local Practice,* edited by S. C. Carr and T. S. Sloan, 19–44. New York: Plenum, 2003.

Pring, Richard. *Personal and Social Education in the Curriculum.* London: Hodder and Stoughton, 1984.

Prior, David. *Jesus Power.* London: Hodder and Stoughton, 1987.

Quimpo, Nathan Gilbert. "Oligarchic Patrimonialism, Bossism, Electoral Clientelism, and Contested Democracy in the Philippines." *Comparative Politics* 37 (2005) 229–50.

Remigio, Amador A., Jr. "A Demographic Survey of the Filipino Diaspora." In *Scattered,* edited by Luis L. Pantoja et al., 5–36. Philippines: LifeChange, 2004.

Royce, Edward. *Poverty and Power: The Problems of Structural Inequality.* New York: Rowman & Littlefield, 2009.

Rynkiewich, Michael. *Soul, Self, and Society.* Eugene, OR: Cascade, 2011.

Samuel, Vinay. "Mission as Transformation." *Transformation* 19 (2002) 243–47.

Samuel, V. and C. Sugden. *Mission as Transformation.* Oxford: Regnum, 1999.

Seamands, Stephen. *Ministry in the Image of God.* Downers Grove, IL: InterVarsity, 2005.

Shaw, Mark. *Doing Theology with Huck and Jim.* Downers Grove, IL: InterVarsity, 1993.

Sidel, John T. *Capital, Coercion, and Crime: Bossism in the Philippines.* Stanford, CA: Stanford University Press, 1999.

Simbulan, Dante. "A Study of the Socio-economic Elite in Philippine Politics and Government, 1946–1963." PhD diss., Australian National University, 1965.

Bibliography

Sloan, Tod S. "Poverty and Psychology: A Call to Arms." In *Poverty and Psychology: From Global Perspective to Local Practice,* edited by S. C. Carr and T. S. Sloan, 301–314. New York: Plenum, 2003.

Sponheim, Paul R. *Love's Availing Power: Imaging God, Imagining the World.* Minneapolis: Fortress, 2011.

Stackhouse, Max L. *Globalization and Grace: Vol. 4 of God and Globalization.* New York: Continuum, 2007.

Stauffer, Robert. "Philippine Democracy: Contradictions of Third World Redemocratization." *Kasarinlan* 6 (1990) 7–22.

Steger, Manfred B. *The Rise of the Global Imaginary.* Oxford: Oxford University Press, 2009.

Stoney, Sierra, and Jeanne Batalova. "Filipino Immigrants in the United States." *Migration Information Source* (Migration Policy Institute), Jeanne (June 5, 2013).

Stravers, David. "Poverty, Conversion, and Worldview in the Philippines." *Missiology: An International Review* 16 (1988) 331–48.

Taylor, Charles. *Modern Social Imaginaries.* Durham and London: Duke University Press, 2004.

———. *A Secular Age.* Cambridge, MA: The Belknap Press of Harvard University Press, 2007.

Teehankee, Julio C. "Clientelism and Party Politics in the Philippines." In *Clientelism and Electoral Competition in Indonesia, Thailand and the Philippines,* edited by Dirk Tomsa and Andreas Ufen, 186–214. Oxford: Routledge, 2012.

Texans One and All by Institute of Texan Cultures. "Filipino Texans." https://texancultures.utsa.edu/wp-content/uploads/2019/08/TxOneAll_FilipinoCombined2019-1.pdf.

Tira, Sadiri Joy, and Enoch Wan. "Filipino Experience in Diaspora Missions: A Case Study of Christian Communities in Contemporary Contexts." *Commission VII: Christian Communities in Contemporary Contexts,* Edinburgh, June 12–13, 2009.

Tuason, Teresa G. "Those Who Were Born Poor: A Qualitative Study of Philippine Poverty." *International Perspectives in Psychology: Research, Practice, Consultation,* 1(S) (2001) 38–57.

Tuason, Ma. Teresa G., et al., "On Both Sides of the Hyphen: Exploring the Filipino-American Identity." *Journal of Counseling Psychology* 54 (2007) 362–72.

United States Census Bureau. "Profile of General Population and Housing Characteristics: 2010." *2010 Census Summary File 2.* https://www.census.gov/history/pdf/2010angelscamp.pdf.

Volf, Miroslav. *A Public Faith: How Followers of Christ Should Serve the Common Good.* Grand Rapids: Brazos, 2011.

Walls, Andrew F. *The Cross-Cultural Process In Christian History.* Maryknoll, NY: Orbis, 2002.

———. "Globalization and the Study of Christian History." In *Globalizing Theology,* edited by Craig Ott and Harold A. Netland. Grand Rapids: Baker, 2006.

Wan, Enoch. "Diaspora Missiology." *Occasional Bulletin* (2007).

———. *Diaspora Missiology: Theory, Methodology, and Practice.* Portland, OR: Institute of Diaspora Studies, 2011.

Wan, Enoch, and Sadiri Joy Tira. "Diaspora Missiology and Missions in the Context of the Twenty-First Century." *Torch Trinity Journal* 13 (2010) 46–60.

————. "The Filipino Experience in Diaspora Missions: a Case Study of Mission Initiatives from the Majority World Churches." *Evangelical Missiological Society-Northwest,* Portland, Oregon, April 5, 2008.

Ward, Keith. "Cosmos and Kenosis." In *The Work of Love: Creation as Kenosis,* edited by John Polkinghorne, 152–66. Grand Rapids: Eerdmans, 2001.

Warner, Stephen R., and J. G. Wittner, eds. *Gatherings in Diaspora: Religious Communities and the New Immigration.* Philadelphia: Temple University Press, 1998.

Weber, Max. *Economy and Society.* Edited by Guenther Roth and Claus Wittich. Berkley, CA: University of California Press, 1968.

————. *Protestant Ethic and the Spirit of Capitalism.* New York: Routledge, 1992.

Wink, Walter. *Engaging the Powers.* Minneapolis: Augsburg Fortress, 1992.

————. *The Powers That Be.* New York: Doubleday, 1998.

Wogaman, Philip. "The Doctrine of God and Dilemmas of Power." In *Trinity, Community and Power,* edited by M. Douglas Meeks, 33–50. Wolfeboro, NH: Kingswood, 2000.

Wolterstorff, Nicholas. *Until Justice and Peace Embrace: The Kuyper Lectures for 1981 Delivered at the Free University of Amsterdam.* Grand Rapids: Eerdmans, 1983.

World Bank. "Income Share Held by Highest 20%." http://data.worldbank.org/indicator/SI.DST.05TH.20/countries.

————. "Migration and Development Brief." http://pubdocs.worldbank.org/en/992371492706371662/MigrationandDevelopmentBrief27.pdf.

Woodberry, Robert D. "The Missionary Roots of Liberal Democracy." *American Political Science Review* 106 (2012) 244–74.

Yancey, George. "An Examination of the Effects of Residential and Church Integration on Racial Attitudes of Whites." *Sociological Perspectives* 42 (1999) 279–304.

Yoder, John Howard. *The Christian Witness to the State, Institute of Mennonite Studies 3.* Newton, KS: Faith and life, 1964.

Index

Index